ISBN 978-1-331-75991-1
PIBN 10231062

Shakespearean Quotations

Subjects Classified and Alphabetically Arranged

Compiled by

Emma M. Rawlins

New York
Published by The Author
148 St. Ann's Avenue
1900

COPYRIGHT, 1898, BY

EMMA M. RAWLINS

TO

H. M. L.

THIS LITTLE BOOK

IS MOST

GRATEFULLY INSCRIBED

PREFATORY NOTE.

The compiler's apology for offering this little work to the public is that, during a wide experience as teacher, she has found great need for such a book of reference.

It is therefore hoped that the convenient size, clear type, and classification of subjects of this manual will recommend it to students of Shakespeare.

All the so-called "Familiar" quotations are given, with many others, which, perhaps, are not so well known.

But few of the selections are more than two lines, thus making them easy to memorize.

An appendix is subjoined, however, for reference to special longer passages.

E. M. R.

CONTENTS

MISCELLANEOUS.

SHAKESPEAREAN QUOTATIONS

ANGELS

Angels and ministers of grace, defend us!
Hamlet.   Act I. Sc. 4.

A ministering angel shall my sister be,
When thou liest howling.
Act V. Sc. 1.

Flights of angels sing thee to thy rest!
Act V. Sc. 2.

O, what may man within him hide,
Though angel on the outward side!
Measure for Measure.   Act III. Sc. 2.

Curse his better angel from his side.
Othello.   Act V. Sc. 2.

           Some holy angel
Fly . . . and unfold
His message ere he come.
Macbeth.   Act III. Sc. 6.

Angels are bright still, though the brightest fell.
Act IV. Sc. 3.

Though this is a heavenly angel, hell is here!
> Cymbeline.   Act II. Sc. 2.

By Jupiter, an angel! or, if not,
An earthly paragon!
> Act III. Sc. 6.

There's not the smallest orb which thou behold'st,
But in his motion like an angel sings.
> Merchant of Venice.   Act V. Sc. 1.

If angels fight,
Weak men must fall, for heaven still guards the
right.
> King Richard II.   Act III. Sc. 2.

And vaulted with such ease into his seat,
As if an angel dropp'd down from the clouds.
> King Henry IV.   Part I.   Act. IV. Sc. 1.

There is a good angel about him.
> Part II.   Act II. Sc. 4.

Consideration, like an angel, came
And whipp'd the offending Adam out of him.
> King Henry V.   Act I. Sc. 1.

Good angels guard thee!
> King Richard III.   Act IV. Sc. 1.

Good angels guard thy battle.
> Act V. Sc. 3.

Ye have angels' faces, but heaven knows your
hearts.
> King Henry VIII.   Act III. Sc. 1.

Now, good angels
Fly o'er thy . . . head, and shade thy person
Under their blessed wings!

Act V. Sc. 1.

AMBITION

Thy ambition,
Thou scarlet sin, robb'd this bewailing land.

King Henry VIII.   Act III. Sc. 2.

I charge thee, fling away ambition:
By that sin fell the angels.

Ibid.

But 'tis a common proof,
That lowliness is young ambition's ladder.

Julius Cæsar.   Act. II. Sc. 1.

When that the poor have cried, Cæsar hath wept:
Ambition should be made of sterner stuff.

Act III. Sc. 2.

I have no spur
To prick the sides of my intent, but only
Vaulting ambition.

Macbeth.   Act 1. Sc. 7.

And ambition,
The soldier's virtue, rather makes choice of loss,
Than gain which darkens him.

Antony and Cleopatra.   Act III. Sc. 1.

Farewell the plumed troop, and the big wars,
That make ambition virtue! O, farewell!

Othello.   Act III. Sc. 3.

BRAIN

O, there has been much throwing about of brains!
Hamlet.   Act II. Sc. 2.

Sleep rock thy brain!
Act III. Sc. 2.

This is the very coinage of your brain.
Act III. Sc. 4.

Cudgel thy brains no more about it.
Act V. Sc. 1.

His pure brain,
Which some suppose the soul's frail dwelling-
house,
Doth by the idle comments that it makes
Foretell the ending of mortality.
King John.   Act V. Sc. 7.

My brain I'll prove the female to my soul,
My soul the father.
King Richard II.   Act V. Sc. 5.

Brain **him** with his lady's fan.
King Henry IV.   Act II. Sc. 3.

My brain more busy than the labouring spider
Weaves tedious snares to trap mine enemies.
King Henry VI.   Part II.   Act III. Sc. 2.

Raze out the written troubles of the brain.
Macbeth.   Act V. Sc. 3.

I talk of dreams,
Which are the children of an idle brain.
Romeo and Juliet.   Act I. Sc. 4.

The brain may devise laws for the blood,
but a hot temper leaps o'er a cold decree.
The Merchant of Venice. Act I. Sc. 2.

Have I laid my brain in the sun and dried it, that
it wants matter to prevent so gross o'er reaching as this?
Merry Wives of Windsor. Act V. Sc. 5.

Shall quips and sentences and these paper bullets
of the brain awe a man from the career of his
humour?
Much Ado About Nothing. Act II. Sc. 3.

If a man will be beaten with brains, a' shall wear
nothing handsome about him.
Act V. Sc. 4.

I have very poor and unhappy brains for
drinking.
Othello. Act II. Sc. 3.

BEAUTY

Then let her beauty be her wedding dower.
Two Gentlemen of Verona. Act III. Sc. 1.

O beauty,
Till now I never knew thee!
King Henry VIII. Act I. Sc. 4.

Beauty is bought by judgment of the eye,
Not utter'd by base sale of chapmen's tongues.
Love's Labour's Lost. Act II. Sc. 1.

O, she is rich in beauty, only poor,
That when she dies with beauty dies her store.
Romeo and Juliet.   Act I. Sc. 1.

Beauty too rich for use, for earth too dear!
Act I. Sc. 5.

Beautiful tyrant! fiend angelical!
Act III. Sc. 2.

Ay, beauty's princely majesty is such,
Confounds the tongue and makes the senses rough.
King Henry VI.   Part I.   Act V. Sc. 3.

'Tis beauty that doth oft make women proud.
Part III.   Act I. Sc. 4.

'Tis beauty truly blent, whose red and white
Nature's own sweet and cunning hand laid on.
Twelfth Night.   Act I. Sc. 5.

For beauty is a witch
Against whose charms faith melteth into blood.
Much Ado About Nothing.   Act II. Sc. 1.

Beauty is but a vain and doubtful good.
Passionate Pilgrim.

BOOK

That book in many's eyes doth share the glory,
That in gold clasps locks in the golden story.
Romeo and Juliet.   Act I. Sc. 3.

You kiss by the book.
Act I. Sc. 5.

One writ with me in sour misfortune's book!
Act V. Sc. 2.

In nature's infinite book of secrecy
A little I can read.
Antony and Cleopatra. Act I. Sc. 2.

Deeper than did ever plummet sound
I'll drown my book.
The Tempest. Act V. Sc. 1.

I had rather than forty shillings I had my
Book of Songs and Sonnets here.
The Merry Wives of Windsor. Act I. Sc. 1.

Small have continual plodders ever won
Save base authority from others' books.
Love's Labour's Lost. Act I. Sc. 1.

Mark'd with a blot, damn'd in the book of heaven.
King Richard II. Act IV. Sc. 1.

I'll read enough,
When I do see the very book indeed,
Where all my sins are writ, and that's myself.
Ibid.

Who hath not heard it spoken
How deep you were within the books of God?
King Henry IV. Part II. Act IV. Sc. 2.

I'll note you in my book of memory.
King Henry VI. Part I. Act II. Sc. 4.

Our forefathers had no other books but the score
and the tally.
Part II. Act IV. Sc. 7.

Made him my book, wherein my soul recorded
The history of all her secret thoughts.
King Richard III.   Act III. Sc. 5.

Books in the running brooks.
As You Like It.   Act II. Sc. 1.

These trees shall be my books
And in their barks my thoughts I'll character.
Act III. Sc. 2.

I see, lady, the gentleman is not in your books.
Much Ado About Nothing.   Act I. Sc. 1.

CONSCIENCE.

So much my conscience whispers in your ear,
Which none but heaven and you and I shall hear.
King John.   Act. I. Sc. 1.

Now, for our consciences, the arms are fair,
When the intent of bearing them is just.
King Henry IV.   Part I.   Act V. Sc. 2.

What you speak is in your conscience wash'd
As pure as sin with baptism.
King Henry V.   Act I. Sc. 2.

And he but naked, though lock'd up in steel,
Whose conscience with injustice is corrupted.
King Henry VI.   Part II.   Act III. Sc. 2.

The worm of conscience still begnaw thy soul!
King Richard III.   Act I. Sec. 3.

Faith, some certain dregs of conscience are yet
within me.
Act I. Sc. 4.

Every man's conscience is a thousand swords.
Act V. Sc. 2.

O, coward conscience, how dost thou afflict me!
Act V. Sc. 3.

My conscience hath a thousand several tongues.
Ibid.

Conscience is but a word that cowards use.
Act V. Sc. 4.

O my . . .
The quiet of my wounded conscience.
King Henry VIII.   Act II. Sc. 2.

It seems the marriage with his brother's wife
Has crept too near his conscience.
Ibid.

No, his conscience
Has crept too near another lady.
King Henry VIII.   Act II. Sc. 2.

But conscience, conscience!
O, 'tis a tender place.
Act II. Sc. 2.

I meant to rectify my conscience.
Act II. Sc. 4.

There's nothing I have done yet, o' my conscience,
Deserves a corner.
Act III. Sc. 1.

A peace above all earthly dignities,
A still and quiet conscience.
Act III. Sc. 2.

Very reverend sport, truly; and done in the testimony of a good conscience.

Love's Labour's Lost.   Act. IV. Sc. 2.

Consciences that will not die in debt.

Act V. Sc. 2.

For policy sits above conscience.

Timon of Athens.   Act III. Sc. 2.

Thus conscience does make cowards of us all.

Hamlet.   Act III. Sc. 1.

Now must your conscience my acquittance seal.

Act IV. Sc. 7.

Is't not perfect conscience,
To quit him with this arm?

Act V. Sc. 2.

A very gentle beast, and of a good conscience.

Midsummer Night's Dream.   Act V. Sc. 1.

Twenty consciences,
That stand 'twixt me and . . . candied be they
And melt ere they molest.

The Tempest.   Act II. Sc. 1.

Therefore is it most expedient for the wise (if
Don Worm, his conscience, find no impediment
To the contrary) to be the trumpet to his own
virtues.

Much Ado About Nothing.   Act V. Sc. 2.

I'll haunt thee like a wicked conscience still,
That mouldeth goblins swift as frenzy's thoughts.

Troilus and Cressida.   Act V. Sc. 10.

COURTESY

How he did seem to dive into their hearts,
With humble and familiar courtesy.
King Richard II. Act I. Sc. 4.

Me rather had my heart might feel your love
Than my unpleased eye see your courtesy.
Act III. Sc. 3.

And then I stole all courtesy from heaven,
And dress'd myself in such humility
That I did pluck allegiance from men's hearts.
King Henry IV. Part I. Act III. Sc. 2.

If a man will make courtesy and say nothing, he
is virtuous.
King Henry IV. Part II. Act II. Sc. 1.

The mirror of all courtesy.
King Henry VIII. Act II. Sc. 1.

I am the very pink of courtesy.
Romeo and Juliet. Act II. Sc. 4.

He is not the flower of courtesy.
Act II. Sc. 5.

In courtesy gives undeserving praise.
Love's Labour's Lost. Act V. Sc. 2.

Why, this is he
That kiss'd his hand away in courtesy.
Ibid.

Courtesy itself must convert to disdain, if you
come in her presence.
Much Ado About Nothing. Act I. Sc. 1.

Then is courtesy a turncoat.
                                        Ibid.

But manhood is melted into courtesies, valour
into compliments.
            Much Ado About Nothing.   Act IV. Sc. 1.

He was wont to lend money for a Christian
courtesy; let him look to his bond.
                Merchant of Venice.   Act III. Sc. 1.

It must appear in other ways than words,
Therefore I scant this breathing courtesy.
                                    Act V. Sc. 1.

I was beset with shame and courtesy.
                                        Ibid.

How courtesy would seem to cover sin!
                    Pericles.   Act I. Sc. 1.

COURAGE.

For courage mounteth with occasion.
                King John.   Act II. Sc. 1.

But screw your courage to the sticking-place,
And we'll not fail.

                        Macbeth.   Act I. Sc. 7.

CUSTOM.

Though I am native here
And to the manner born, it is a custom
More honour'd in the breach than the observance.
                    Hamlet.   Act I. Sc. 4.

Sleeping within my orchard,
My custom always of the afternoon.
                                    Act I. Sc. 5.

Nature her custom holds,
Let shame say what it will.
                                    Act IV. Sc. 7.

Custom hath made it in him a property of easi-
ness.
                                    Act V. Sc. 1.

Age can not wither her, not custom stale
Her infinite variety.
            Antony and Cleopatra.   Act II. Sc. 2.

Think of this . . . .
But as a thing of custom, 'tis no other;
Only it spoils the pleasure of the time.
                    Macbeth.   Act III. Sc. 4.

Nice customs curtsey to great kings.
                    King Henry V.   Act V. Sc. 2.

CURSE

The common curse of mankind, folly and ignorance, be thine in great revenue!
                Troilus and Cressida.   Act II Sc. 3.

'Tis the curse of service
Preferment goes by letter and affection,
And not by old gradation.
                    Othello.   Act I. Sc. 1.

O curse of marriage,
That we can call these delicate creatures ours,
And not their appetites!

> Act III. Sc. 3.

Dreading the curse that money may buy out;
And by the merit of vile gold, dross, dust,
Purchase corrupted pardon of a man.

> King John.   Act III. Sc. 1.

Can curses pierce the clouds and enter heaven?
Why, then, give way, dull clouds, to my quick
    curses!

> King Richard III.   Act I. Sc. 3.

Their curses now
Live where their prayers did.

> King Henry VIII.   Act I. Sc. 2.

Curses, not loud but deep.

> Macbeth.   Act V. Sc. 3.

Cursed be he that moves my bones.

> Shakespeare's Epitaph.

CALUMNY

Be thou as chaste as ice, as pure as snow, thou
shalt not escape calumny.

> Hamlet.   Act III. Sc. 1.

No might nor greatness in mortality
Can censure 'scape; back-wounding calumny.

> Measure for Measure.   Act III. Sc. 2.

CAPTAIN

And there at Venice gave
His body to that pleasant country's earth,
And his pure soul unto his captain, Christ.
King Richard II.   Act IV. Sc. 1.

O Thou, whose captain I account myself,
Look on my forces with a gracious eye.
King Richard III.   Act V. Sc. 3.

That in the captain 's but a choleric word,
Which in the soldier is flat blasphemy.
Measure for Measure.   Act II. Sc. 2.

Who does i' the wars more than his captain can,
Becomes his captain's captain.
Antony and Cleopatra.   Act III. Sc. 1.

O, he is the courageous captain of compliments!
Romeo and Juliet.   Act II.-Sc. 4.

CUPID

If we can do this, Cupid is no longer an archer.
Much Ado About Nothing.   Act II. Sc. 1.

Of this matter
Is little Cupid's crafty arrow made,
That only wounds by hearsay.
Act III. Sc. 1.

Some Cupid kills with arrows, some with traps.
Ibid.

He hath twice or thrice cut
Cupid's bow-string, and the little hangman dare
not shoot at him.   Act III. Sc. 2.

Cupid is a knavish lad,
Thus to make poor females mad.
                Midsummer Night's Dream.   Act III. Sc. 2.

Dian's bud o'er Cupid's flower
Hath such force and blessed power.
                                        Act IV. Sc. 1.

He is Cupid's grandfather and learns news of
    him.   Love's Labour's Lost.   Act II. Sc. 1.

Saint Cupid, then!   Act IV. Sc. 3.

She'll not be hit
With Cupid's arrow: she hath Dian's wit.
                Romeo and Juliet.   Act I. Sc. 1.

Why, now is Cupid a child of conscience; he
    makes restitution.
                Merry Wives of Windsor.   Act V. Sc. 5.

For I long to see
Quick Cupid's post that comes so mannerly.
                The Merchant of Venice.   Act II. Sc. 9.

He that will divide a minute into a thousand
    parts and break but a part of the thousandth
    part of a minute in the affairs of love, it may
    be said of him that Cupid hath clapp'd him o'
    the shoulder, but I'll warrant him heart whole.
                As You Like It.   Act IV. Sc. 1.

Young Adam Cupid, he that shot so trim,
When King Cophetua loved the beggar maid!
                Romeo and Juliet.   Act II. Sc. 1.

CANDLE

How far that little candle throws his beams!
So shines a good deed in a naughty world.
                The Merchant of Venice.   Act V. Sc. 1.

By these blessed candles of the night.
                                Ibid.

Night's candles are burned out, and jocund day
Stands tiptoe on the misty mountain tops.
                Romeo and Juliet.   Act III. Sc. 5.

There's husbandry in heaven;
Their candles are all out.
                Macbeth.   Act II. Sc. 1.

Out, out, brief candle!
                Act V. Sc. 5.

COWARD

We'll have a swashing and a martial outside
As many other mannish cowards have.
                As You Like It.   Act I. Sc. 3.

Cowards father cowards and base things sire base.
                Cymbeline.   Act IV. Sc. 2.

A plague of all cowards!
        King Henry IV.   Part I.   Act II. Sc. 4.

I was now a coward on instinct.
                                Ibid.

DEATH

O, now doth death line his dead chaps with steel.
King John.   Act II. Sc. 1.

Death, death; O amiable lovely death!
Act III. Sc. 4.

O death, made proud with pure and princely beauty!
Act IV. Sc. 3.

'Tis strange that death should sing.
Act V. Sc. 7.

And nothing can we call our own but death.
King Richard II.   Act III. Sc. 2.

I were better to be eaten to death with a rust than to be scoured to nothing with perpetual motion.
King Henry IV.   Part II.   Act I. Sc. 2.

Just death, kind umpire of men's miseries,
With sweet enlargement doth dismiss me hence.
King Henry VI.   Part I.   Act II. Sc. 5.

Thou antic death, which laugh'st us here to scorn!
Act IV. Sc. 7.

Ah, what sign it is of evil life,
Where death's approach is seen so terrible!
Part II.   Act III. Sc. 3.

The worst is death; and death will have his day.
King Richard III.   Act III. Sc. 2.

The sense of death is most in apprehension.
Measure for Measure.   Act III. Sc. 1.

Av. but to die, and go we know not where.

ERRATA.

P. 26, bottom line for Richard " III." read " II."

P. 40, line 10 from top for Sc. " 5 " read " 15."

P. 40, line 15 from top for Sc. " 3 " read " 2."

P. 42, line 2 from top for Sc. " 1 " read " 3."

P. 98, line 9 from top for Sc. " 2 " read " 1."

P. 102, line 7 from top for Part " II." read " I."

P. 112, line 5 from top for Sc. " 1 " read " 2."

P. 114, line 8 from bottom for Sc. " 1 " read " 2."

P. 114, bottom line for Sc. " 2 " read " 1."

P. 124, line 11 from top for " Othello " read " Macbeth

P. 142, line 6 from top for " III." read " V."

P. 143, line 7 from top for Sc. " 2 " read " 7."

P. 154, line 3 from top for Act " III." read " II."

Death, that hath suck'd the honey of thy breath,
Hath had no power yet upon thy beauty.
Act V. Sc. 2.

DEATH

O, now doth death line his dead chaps with steel.
King John.   Act II. Sc. 1.

I.

Part II.   Act III. Sc. 3.

The worst is death; and death will have his day.
King Richard III.   Act III. Sc. 2.

The sense of death is most in apprehension.
Measure for Measure. Act III. Sc. 1.

Ay, but to die, and go we know not where.
Ibid.

Be absolute for death: either death or life
Shall thereby be the sweeter.
Measure for Measure. Act III. Sc. 1.

Yet in this life
Lie hid more thousand deaths, yet death we fear,
That makes these odds all even.
Ibid.

O, death's a great disguiser!
Act IV. Sc. 2.

When beggars die there are no comets seen;
The heavens themselves blaze forth the death of
princes.
Julius Cæsar. Act II. Sc. 2.

It seems to me most strange that men should fear:
Seeing that death, a necessary end,
Will come when it will come.
Ibid.

Death lies on her like an untimely frost
Upon the sweetest flower of all the field.
Romeo and Juliet. Act IV. Sc. 5.

Death, that hath suck'd the honey of thy breath,
Hath had no power yet upon thy beauty.
Act V. Sc. 2.

I would fain die a dry death.
                    The Tempest.   Act I. Sc. 1.

He that dies pays all debts.
                         Act III. Sc. 2.

Death, that dark spirit, in's nervy arm doth lie;
Which, being advanced, declines, and then men
    die.
                    Coriolanus.   Act II. Sc. 1.

Out of the jaws of death.
                    Twelfth Night.   Act III. Sc. 4.

Done to death by slanderous tongues.
            Much Ado About Nothing.   Act V. Sc. 3.

Speak me fair in death.
            Merchant of Venice.   Act IV. Sc. 1.

For death remember'd should be like a mirror,
Who tells us life's but breath, to trust it error.
                    Pericles.   Act I. Sc. 1.

DAGGER

                    Art thou but
        A dagger of the mind?
                    Macbeth.   Act II. Sc. 1.

There's daggers in men's smiles.
                         Act II. Sc. 3.

This is the air-drawn dagger.
                         Act III. Sc. 4.

She speaks poniards, and every word stabs.
                Much Ado About Nothing.   Act II. Sc. 1.

Hath no man's dagger here a point for me?
                                Act IV. Sc. 1.

I will speak daggers to her, but use none.
                Hamlet.   Act III. Sc. 2.

These words, like daggers, enter in mine ears.
                                Act III. Sc. 4.

                        For I wear not
My dagger in my mouth.
                        Cymbeline.   Act IV. Sc. 2.

Thou hidest a thousand daggers in thy thoughts!
                King Henry IV.   Part II.   Act IV. Sc. 5.

DEVIL

Some airy devil hovers in the sky
And pours down mischief.
                        King John.   Act III. Sc. 2.

He will give the devil his due.
                King Henry IV.   Part I.   Act I. Sc. 2.

Tell truth and shame the devil.
                                Act III. Sc. 1.

            You are mortal,
And mortal eyes can not endure the devil.
                King Richard III.   Act I. Sc. 2.

The devil hath power
To assume a pleasing shape.
                        Hamlet.   Act II. Sc. 2.

With devotion's visage
And pious action we do sugar o'er
The devil himself.

Act III. Sc. 1.

The devil can cite Scriptures for his purpose.

The Merchant of Venice.   Act I. Sc. 3.

He must needs go that the devil drives.

All's Well That Ends Well.   Act. I. Sc. 3.

'Tis the eye of childhood
That fears a painted devil.

Macbeth.   Act II. Sec. 2.

Every
Inordinate cup is unblessed, and the ingredient
is a devil.

Othello.   Act II. Sec. 3.

He must have a long spoon that must eat with
the devil.

The Comedy of Errors.   Act IV. Sc. 4.

Devils soonest tempt, resembling spirits of light.

Love's Labour's Lost.   Act IV. Sc. 3.

DIVINITY

There's such divinity doth hedge a king,
That treason can but peep to what it would.

Hamlet.   Act. IV. Sc. 5.

There's a divinity that shapes our ends,
Rough-hew them how we will.

Act V. Sc. 2.

They say there is divinity in odd numbers,
either in nativity, chance, or death.
Merry Wives of Windsor. Act V. Sc. 1.

DOUBTS

Our doubts are traitors
And make us lose the good we oft might win
By fearing to attempt.
Measure for Measure. Act I. Sc. 4.

But now I am cabin'd, cribb'd, confined, bound
in
To saucy doubts and fears.
Macbeth. Act III. Sc. 4.

Modest doubt is call'd
The beacon of the wise.
Troilus and Cressida. Act. II. Sc. 2.

DOGS

I had rather be a dog and bay the moon,
Than such a Roman.
Julius Cæsar. Act IV. Sc. 3.

Hounds. and grayhounds, mongrels, spaniels,
curs,
Shoughs, water-rugs, and demi-wolves, are clept
All by the name of dogs.
Macbeth. Act III. Sc. 1.

If I want gold, steal but a beggar's dog,
And give it Timon, why, the dog coins gold.
Timon of Athens. Act II. Sc. 1.

I had rather be a beggar's dog than Apemantus.
Act IV. Sc. 3.

Give to dogs
What thou deny'st to men.
Ibid.

I had rather hear my dog bark at a crow than a man swear he loves me.
Much Ado About Nothing.   Act I. Sc. 1.

And he had been a dog that should have howled thus, they would have hanged him.
Act II. Sc. 3.

Make them of no more voice
Than dogs that are as often beat for barking
As, therefore, kept to do so.
Coriolanus.   Act II. Sc. 3.

I have dogs   .   .   .
Will rouse the proudest panther in the chase.
Titus Andronicus.   Act II. Sc. 2.

The little dogs and all,
Tray, Blanch, and Sweetheart, too, see they bark at me.
King Lear.   Act III. Sc. 6.

ENEMY

O God, that men should put an enemy in their mouths to steal away their brains!
Othello.   Act II. Sc. 3.

'Tis death to me to be at enmity.
King Richard III.   Act II. Sc. 1.

A thing devised by the enemy.
Act V. Sc. 3.

He would not in mine age
Have left me naked to mine enemies.
King Henry VIII.   Act III. Sc. 2.

Mine enemy's dog,
Though he had bit me, should have stood that
night
Against my fire.
King Lear.   Act IV. Sc. 7.

In cases of defence 'tis best to weigh
The enemy more mighty than he seems.
King Henry V.   Act II. Sc. 4.

I am sure care 's an enemy to life.
Twelfth Night.   Act I. Sc. 3.

Security
Is mortals' chiefest enemy.
Macbeth.   Act III. Sc. 5.

EARTH

I'l put a girdle round about the earth
In forty minutes.
Midsummer Night's Dream.   Act II. Sc. 1.

For naught so vile that on the earth doth live,
But to the earth some special good doth give.
Romeo and Juliet.   Act II. Sc. 3.

"Give him a little earth for charity. "
King Henry VIII.   Act IV. Sc. 2.

O, pardon me, thou bleeding piece of earth,
That I am meek and gentle with these butchers!
Julius Cæsar.   Act III. Sc. 1.

The earth has bubbles, as the water has,
And these are of them.
Macbeth.   Act I. Sc. 3.

FRIENDS

Call you that backing of your friends?   A plague
upon such backing!
King Henry IV.   Part I.   Act II. Sc. 4.

And all my friends which thou must make thy
friends
Have but their stings and teeth newly ta'en out.
Part II.   Act IV. Sc. 5.

God keep me from false friends!
King Richard III.   Act III. Sc. 1.

For those you make friends
And give your hearts to, when they once per-
ceive
The least rub in your fortunes, fall away
Like water from ye.
King Henry VIII.   Act II. Sc. 1.

I am wealthy in my friends.
                Timon of Athens.   Act II. Sc. 2.

                        All gone! and not
One friend to take his fortune by the arm,
And go along with him!
                        Act IV. Sc. 2.

What viler thing upon the earth than friends
Who can bring noblest minds to basest ends!
                        Act IV. Sc. 3.

    Neither a borrower nor a lender be :
For loan oft loses both itself and friend.
                    Hamlet.   Act I. Sc. 3.

Those friends thou hast and their adoption tried,
Grapple them to thy soul with hoops of steel.
                        Act I. Sc. 3.

    Who in want a hollow friend doth try,
    Directly seasons him his enemy.
                        Act III. Sc. 2.

For who not needs shall never lack a friend.
                        Ibid.

He that wants money, means and content is
without three good friends.
                As You Like It.   Act III. Sc. 2.

A friend should bear his friend's infirmities,
But Brutus makes mine greater than they are.
                Julius Cæsar.   Act IV. Sc. 3.

This passion, and the death of a dear friend, would go near to make a man look sad.
Midsummer Night's Dream. Act V. Sc. 1.

And do as adversaries do in law,
Strive mightily, but eat and drink as friends.
Taming of the Shrew. Act I. Sc. 2.

My friends were poor, but honest.
All's Well That Ends Well. Act I. Sc. 3.

Now I dare not say I have one friend alive.
The Two Gentlemen of Verona. Act V. Sc. 4.

We have no friend
But resolution, and the briefest end.
Antony and Cleopatra. Act IV. Sc. 15.

He that is thy friend, indeed,
He will help thee in thy need.
The Passionate Pilgrim.

Every man will be thy friend,
Whilst thou hast wherewith to spend.
Ibid.

Left and abandon'd of his velvet friends.
As You Like It. Act II. Sc. 1.

Lose not so noble a friend on vain suppose,
Nor with sour looks afflict his noble heart.
Titus Andronicus. Act I. Sc. 1.

FAULTS

O, what a world of vile ill-favour'd faults
Looks handsome in three hundred pounds a year!
Merry Wives of Windsor. Act III. Sc. 4.

Condemn the fault, and not the actor of it?
Measure for Measure. Act II. Sc. 2.

That we were all, as some would seem to be,
Free from our faults, as from faults seeming free!
Measure for Measure. Act III. Sc. 2

'Tis a fault to heaven,
A fault against the dead, a fault to nature,
To reason most absurd.
Hamlet. Act I. Sc. 2.

Every man has his fault, and honesty is his.
Timon of Athens. Act III. Sc. 1.

And oftentimes excusing of a fault
Doth make the fault the worse by the excuse.
King John. Act IV. Sc. 2.

The image of a wicked heinous fault
Lives in his eye.
Ibid.

The fault, dear Brutus, is not in our stars,
But in ourselves, that we are underlings.
Julius Cæsar. Act I. Sc. 2.

All his faults observed,
Set in a note-book, learn'd, and conn'd by rote.
Act IV. Sc. 3.

Every one fault seeming monstrous till his fellow-
,fault came to match it.
As You Like It.   Act III. Sc. 2.

FORTUNE

Fortune reigns in gifts of the world.
As You Like It.   Act 1. Sc. 2.

One out of suits with fortune.
Ibid.

My pride fell with my fortunes.
Ibid.

Let us sit and mock the good housewife
Fortune from her wheel.
Ibid.

And rail'd on Lady Fortune in good terms.
Act II. Sc. 7.

Fortune shall cull forth
Out of one side her happy minion.
King John.   Act II. Sc. 1.

When Fortune means to men most good,
She looks upon them with a threatening eye.
Act III. Sc. 4.

Will Fortune never come with both hands full?
King Henry IV.   Part II.   Act IV. Sc. 4.

And giddy Fortune's furious fickle wheel.
King Henry V.   Act III. Sc. 6.

Yield not thy neck
To fortune's yoke, but let thy dauntless mind
Still ride in triumph over all mischance.
King Henry VI.   Part III.   Act III. Sc. 3.

Though Fortune's malice overthrow my state,
My mind exceeds the compass of her wheel.
Part III.   Act IV. Sc. 4.

But stoop with patience to my fortune.
Part III.   Act V. Sc. 5.

Fortune is merry,
And in this mood will give us anything.
Julius Cæsar.   Act III. Sc. 2.

There is a tide in the affairs of men,
Which, taken at the flood, leads on to fortune.
Act IV. Sc. III.

I'd whistle her off and let her down the wind,
To prey at fortune.
Othello.   Act. III. Sc. 3.

On Fortune's cap we are not the very button.
Hamlet.   Act II. Sc. 2.

Now the fair goddess Fortune,
Fall deep in love with thee!
Coriolanus.   Act I. Sc. 5.

Well, if Fortune be a woman,
she's a good wench for this gear.
Merchant of Venice.   Act II. Sc. 2.

No, let me speak; and let me rail so high,
That the false housewife Fortune break her wheel,
Provok'd by my offence.
Antony and Cleopatra.   Act IV. Sc. 5.

Fortune brings in some boats that are not steer'd.
Cymbeline.   Act V. Sc. 3.

He shall not knit a knot in his fortunes with the
finger of my substance.
Merry Wives of Windsor.   Act III. Sc. 3.

FOOLS

Thus we play the fools with the time, and the
spirits of the wise sit in the clouds and mock us.
King Henry IV.   Part II.   Act II. Sc. 2.

How ill white hairs become a fool and jester!
King Henry IV.   Part II.   Act V. Sc. 5.

" A fool's bolt is soon shot."
King Henry V. Act III. Sc. 7.

The dullness of the fool is the whetstone of the wits.

> As You Like It.   Act I. Sec. 2.

The more pity, that fools may not speak wisely what wise men do foolishly.

> Ibid.

The little foolery that wise men have makes a great show.

> Ibid.

A fool, a fool! I met a fool i' the forest,
A motley fool.

> Act II. Sc. 7.

My lungs began to grow like chanticleer,
That fools should be so deep contemplative.

> Ibid.

I had rather have a fool to make me merry than experience to make me sad.

> Act IV. Sc. 1.

The fool doth think he is wise, but the wise man knows himself to be a fool.

> Act V. Sc. 1.

Here comes a pair of very strange beasts, which in all tongues are called fools.

> Act V. Sc. 4.

O, these deliberate fools!
> Merchant of Venice.   Act II. Sc. 9.

This is the fool that lent out money gratis.
Merchant of Venice.   Act III. Sc. 1.

Folly in fools bears not so strong a note
As foolery in the wise when wit doth dote.
Love's Labour's Lost.   Act V. Sc. 2.

Thou art the cap of all the fools alive.
Timon of Athens.   Act IV. Sc. 3.

Lord, what fools these mortals be!
Midsummer Night's Dream.   Act III. Sc. 2.

FASHION

Poor I am stale, a garment out of fashion.
Cymbeline.   Act III. Sc. 4.

Let's do it after the high Roman fashion.
Antony and Cleopatra.   Act IV. Sc. 15.

He wears his faith but as the fashion of his hat.
Much Ado About Nothing.   Act I. Sc. 1.

Now will he lie ten nights awake, carving the
fashion of a new doublet.
Act II. Sc. 3.

The fashion wears out more apparel than the man.
Act III. Sc. 3.

Thou art not for the fashion of these times,
Where none will sweat but for promotion.
As You Like It.   Act II. Sc. 3.

A man in all the world's new fashion planted,
That hath a mint of phrases in his brain.
Love's Labour's Lost.   Act I. Sc. 1.

FANCY

Chewing the food of sweet and bitter fancy.
As You Like It.   Act IV. Sc. 3.

And the imperial votaress passed on,
In maiden meditation, fancy-free.
Midsummer Night's Dream.   Act II. Sc. 1.

All impediments in fancy's course,
Are motives of more fancy.
All's Well That Ends Well.   Act V. Sc. 3.

Tell me where is fancy bred,
Or in the heart or in the head?
The Merchant of Venice.   Act. III. Sc. 2.

FATES

Our wills and fates do so contrary run
That our devices still are overthrown.
Hamlet.   Act III. Sc. 2.

Men at some time are masters of their fates.
Julius Cæsar.   Act I. Sc. 2.

But yet I'll make assurance double sure,
And take a bond of fate.

Macbeth.   Act IV. Sc. 1.

O God! that one might read the book of fate!

King Henry IV.   Part II.   Act III. Sc. 1.

I and my fellows
Are ministers of Fate.

The Tempest.   Act III. Sc. 3.

FLATTERY

But when I tell him he hates flatterers,
He says he does, being then most flattered.

Julius Cæsar.   Act II. Sc. 1.

He that loves to be flattered is worthy o' the
flatterer.

Timon of Athens.   Act I. Sc. 1.

Thou flatter'st misery.

Act IV. Sc. 3.

"There is flattery in friendship."

King Henry V.   Act III. Sc. 7.

He would not flatter Neptune for his trident,
Or Jove for 's power to thunder.

Coriolanus.   Act III. Sc. 1.

GOD

God and our right!
King John. Act II. Sc. 1.

God in thy good cause make thee prosperous.
King Richard II. Act I. Sc. 3.

God save the mark!
King Henry IV. Part I. Act I. Sc. 3.

God made him, and therefore let him pass for a man.
The Merchant of Venice. Act I. Sc. 2.

You have the grace of God, ... and he hath enough.
Act II. Sc. 2.

God send every one their heart's desire!
Much Ado About Nothing. Act III. Sc. 4.

God defend but God should go before such villains!
Act IV. Sc. 2.

God grant us patience.
Love's Labour's Lost. Act I. Sc. 1.

GRIEF

For grief is proud and makes his owner stoop.
King John.   Act III. Sc. 1.

For my grief's so great
That no supporter but the huge firm earth
Can hold it up.
Ibid.

The fire is dead with grief.
Act IV. Sc. 1.

Our griefs, and not our manners, reason now.
Sc. 3.

But grief makes one hour ten.
King Richard II.   Act I. Sc. 3.

Thy grief is but thy absence for a time.
Joy absent, grief is present for that time.
Ibid.

Within me grief hath kept a tedious fast.
Act II. Sc. 1.

Each substance of a grief hath twenty shadows.
Sc. 2.

O that I were as great
As is my grief, or lesser than my name!
Act III. Sc. 3.

Drinking my griefs whilst you mount up on high.
Act IV. Sc. 1.

'Tis very true, my grief lies all within ;
And these external manners of laments
Are merely shadows to the unseen grief.
Ibid.

But that still use of grief makes wild grief tame.
King Richard III.   Act IV. Sc. 4.

Every one can master a grief but he that has it.
Much Ado About Nothing.   Act III. Sc. 2.

Being that I flow in grief,
The smallest twine may lead me.
Act IV. Sc. 1.

Patch grief with proverbs.
Act V. Sc. 1.

My griefs cry louder than advertisements.
Ibid.

Some griefs are med'cinable.
Cymbeline.   Act III. Sc. 2.

Triumphs for nothing and lamenting toys
Is jollity for apes and grief for boys.
Act IV.   Sc. 2.

O, grief hath changed me since you saw me last.
The Comedy of Errors.   Act. V. Sc. 1.

My grief lies onward and my joy behind.
Sonnet L.

This grief is crowned with consolation.
Antony and Cleopatra.   Act I. Sc. 2.

I have
That honorable grief lodged here which burns
Worse than tears drown.
The Winter's Tale.   Act II. Sc. 1.

Some grief shows much of love,
But much of grief shows still some want of wit.
Romeo and Juliet.   Act III. Sc. 5.

'Tis unmanly grief:
It shows a will most incorrect to heaven.
Hamlet.   Act I. Sc. 2.

Extremity of griefs would make men mad.
Titus Andronicus.   Act IV. Sc. 1.

GHOST

Never, O never, do his ghost the wrong
To hold your honour more precise and nice
With others than with him!
King Henry IV.   Part II.   Act II. Sc. 3.

Vex not his ghost; O, let him pass! he hates
    him much
That would upon the rack of this tough world
Stretch him out longer.
King Lear.   Act V.   Sc. 3.

By heaven, I'll make a ghost of him that lets me!
Hamlet.   Act I. Sc. 4.

Remember thee!
Ay, thou poor ghost, while memory holds a seat
In this distracted globe.

Act I. Sc. 5.

GOING

Nay, pray you, seek no colour for your going
But, bid farewell, and go.

Antony and Cleopatra.   Act I. Sc. 3.

Stand not upon the order of your going,
But go at once.

Macbeth.   Act III. Sc. 4.

GOLD

All that glisters is not gold.

The Merchant of Venice.   Act II. Sc. 7.

Saint-seducing gold.

Romeo and Juliet.   Act I. Sc. 1.

There is thy gold, worse poison to men's souls,
Doing more murders in this loathsome world,
Than these poor compounds that thou mayst not
sell.

Act V. Sc. 1.

'Tis gold
Which buys admittance.
          Cymbeline.   Act II. Sc. 3.

'Tis gold
Which makes the true man kill'd and
Saves the thief.
                    Ibid.

You yourself
Are much condemn'd to have an itching palm;
To sell and mart your offices for gold
To undeservers.
          Julius Cæsar.   Act IV. Sc. 3.

GIFTS.

Seven hundred pounds and possibilities is goot
    gifts.
          The Merry Wives of Windsor.   Act I. Sc. 1.

Rich gifts wax poor when givers prove unkind.
          Hamlet.   Act III. Sc. 1.

If ladies be but young and fair,
They have the gift to know it.
          As You Like It.   Act II. Sc. 7.

Win her with gifts, if she respect not words.
          Two Gentlemen of Verona.   Act III. Sc. 1.

HEARTS

If heart's presages be not vain,
We three here part that ne'er shall met again.
King Richard II. Act II. Sc. 2.

For I will ease my heart,
Albeit I make a hazard of my head.
King Henry IV. Part I. Act I. Sc. 3.

An habitation giddy and unsure
Hath he that buildeth on the vulgar heart.
Part II. Act I. Sc. 3.

A good heart 's worth gold.
Part II. Act II. Sc. 4.

A heart unspotted is not easily daunted.
King Henry VI. Part II. Act III. Sc. 1.

What stronger breastplate than a heart untainted!
Sc. 2.

Cherish those hearts that hate thee.
King Henry VIII. Act III. Sc. 2.

With a proud heart he wore his humble weeds.
Coriolanus. Act II. Sc. 3.

I have a heart as little apt as yours,
But yet a brain that leads my use of anger
To better vantage.
Act III. Sc. 2.

Your heart's desires be with you!
As You Like It. Act I. Sc. 2.

She may wear her heart out first.
Much Ado About Nothing.   Act II. Sc. 3.

God send every one their heart's desire!
Act III. Sc. 4.

O serpent heart, hid with a flowering face!
Romeo and Juliet.   Act III. Sc. 2.

A heavy heart bears not a nimble tongue.
Love's Labour's Lost.   Act V. Sc. 2.

A light heart lives long.
Ibid.

The valiant heart is not whipt out of his trade.
Measure for Measure.   Act II. Sc. 1.

Better a little chiding than a great deal of heart-
break.
Merry Wives of Windsor.   Act. V. Sc. 2.

My heart prays for him, though my tongue do
curse.
Comedy of Errors.   Act IV. Sc. 2.

My heart
Is true as steel.
Midsummer Night's Dream.   Act II. Sc. 1.

But break, my heart; for I must hold my tongue.
Hamlet.   Act I. Sc. 2.

Let me wring your heart.
                                    Act III. Sc. 4.

I will wear my heart upon my sleeve
For daws to peck at.
                                    Othello. Act I. Sc. 1.

HEAVEN

Heaven lay not my transgression to my charge!
                                    King John. Act I. Sc. 1.

O, let thy vow
First made to heaven, first be to heaven perform'd!
                                    Act III. Sc. 1.

The breath of heaven has blown his spirit out
And strew'd repentant ashes on his head.
                                    Act IV. Sc. 1.

The sun of heaven methought was loath to set,
But stay'd and made the western welkin blush.
                                    Act V. Sc. 4.

Withhold thine indignation, mighty heaven,
And tempt us not to bear above our power!
                                    Act V. Sc. 6.

Let heaven revenge ; for I may never lift
An angry arm against His minister.
                                    King Richard II. Act I. Sc. 2.

Comfort 's in heaven ; and we are on the earth,
Where nothing lives but crosses, cares and grief.
Act II. Sc. 2.

But heaven hath a hand in these events,
To whose high will we bound our calm contents.
Act V. Sc. 2.

He finds the joys of heaven here on earth.
The Merchant of Venice.   Act. III. Sc. 5.

Then
In reason he should never come to heaven.
Ibid.

Heaven doth with us as we with torches do,
Not light them for themselves.
Measure for Measure.   Act I. Sc. 2.

Shall we serve heaven
With less respect than we do minister
To our gross selves?
Measure for Measure.   Act II. Sc. 2.

Heaven hath my empty words : . . .
Heaven in my mouth; . . .
And in my heart the strong and swelling evil
Of my conception.
Act II. Sc. 4.

He who the sword of heaven will bear,
Should be as holy as severe.
Act III. Sc. 2.

O heaven, the vanity of wretched fools!
Act V. Sc. 1.

She wish'd
That heaven had made her such a man.
Othello.   Act I. Sc. 3.

The grace of heaven,
Before, behind thee, and on every hand,
Enwheel thee round!
Act II. Sc. 1.

Look how the floor of heaven
Is thick inlaid with patines of bright gold.
The Merchant of Venice.   Act V. Sc. 1.

He will make the face of heaven so fine
That all the world will be in love with night.
Romeo and Juliet.   Act III. Sc. 2.

The heavens do lour upon you for some ill;
Move them no more by crossing their high will.
Act IV. Sc. 5.

Heaven make you better than your thoughts!
Merry Wives of Windsor.   Act III. Sc. 3.

O heaven, can you hear a good man groan
And not relent, or compassion him ?
Titus Andronicus.   Act IV. Sc. 1.

HONOUR

And if his name be George, I'll call him Peter;
For new made honour doth forget men's names.
King John. Act I. Sc. 1.

A foot of honour better than I was:
But many a many foot of land the worse.
Ibid.

Honour pricks me on.   Yea, but how if honour
   prick me off when I come on? how then?
Can honour set to a leg?   No: or an arm?
No: or take away the grief of a wound?   No.
King Henry IV. Part I. Act V. Sc. 1.

Honour hath no skill in surgery then?   No.
What is honour? A word.
Ibid.

And sounded all the depths and shoals of honour,
Found thee a way, out of his wreck, to rise in.
King Henry VIII. Act III. Sc. 2.

He gave his honours to the world again,
His blessed part to heaven, and slept in peace.
Act IV. Sc. 2.

And those about her
From her shall read the perfect ways of honour.
Act V. Sc. 6.

Set honour in one eye and death i' the other,
And I will look on both indifferently.
Julius Cæsar. Act I. Sc. 2.

For let the gods so speed me as I love
The name of honour more than I fear death.
Ibid.

Well, honour is the subject of my story.
Ibid.

Believe me for mine honour, and have respect
to mine honour, that you may believe.
Act III. Sc. 2.

And as the sun breaks through the darkest
clouds,
So honour peereth in the meanest habit.
Taming of the Shrew. Act IV. Sc. 3.

I, I, I myself sometimes, leaving the fear of God
on the left hand and hiding mine honour in
my necessity, am fain to shuffle.
Merry Wives of Windsor. Act II. Sc. 2.

INGRATITUDE

Ingratitude, thou marble-hearted fiend,
More hideous when thou show'st thee in a child
Than the sea monster!
King Lear. Act I. Sc. 4.

How sharper than a serpent's tooth it is
To have a thankless child!
Ibid.

Pray to the gods to intermit the plague
That needs must light on this ingratitude.
Julius Cæsar.   Act I. Sc. I.

Ingratitude, more strong than traitors' arms,
Quite vanquish'd him.
Act III. Sc. 2.

O, see the monstrousness of man
When he looks out in an ungrateful shape!
Timon of Athens.   Act III. Sc. 2.

He 's flung in rage from this ingrateful seat
Of monstrous friends.
Act IV. Sc. 2.

I am rapt and can not cover
The monstrous bulk of this ingratitude
With any size of words.
Act V. Sc. I.

Ingratitude is monstrous, and for the multitude to be ingrateful, were to make a monster
of the multitude.
Coriolanus.   Act II. Sc. 3.

I hate ingratitude more in a man
Than lying, vainness, babbling drunkenness,
Or any taint of vice whose strong corruption
Inhabits our frail blood.
Twelfth Night.   Act III. Sc. 4.

IMAGINATION

The lunatic, the lover, and the poet
Are of imagination all compact.
Midsummer Night's Dream.   Act V. Sc. 1.

And as imagination bodies forth
The forms of things unknown, the poet's pen
Turns them to shapes and gives to airy nothing
A local habitation and a name.
Ibid.

Such tricks hath strong imagination.
That, if it would but apprehend some joy
It comprehends some bringer of that joy
Ibid.

INNOCENCE

Look like the innocent flower,
But be the serpent under 't.
Macbeth.   Act I. Sc. 5.

The silence often of pure innocence
Persuades when speaking fails.
The Winter's Tale.   Act II. Sc. 2.

Innocence shall make
False accusation blush, and tyranny
Tremble at patience.
Act III. Sc. 2.

INK

Let there be gall enough in thy ink,
Though thou write with a goose-pen.
Twelfth Night.   Act III. Sc. 2.

Taunt him with the license of ink.
Ibid.

Never durst poet touch a pen to write
Until his ink were temper'd with love's sighs.
Love's Labour's Lost.   Act IV. Sc. 3.

He hath not eat paper, as it were; he hath not
drunk ink.
Act IV. Sc. 2.

Beauteous as ink.
Act V. Sc. 2.

O, she is fallen
Into a pit of ink, that the wide sea
Hath drops too few to wash her clean again.
Much Ado About Nothing.   Act IV. Sc. 1.

JEALOUSY

Trifles light as air
Are to the jealous confirmation strong
As proofs of holy writ.
Othello.   Act. III. Sc. 3.

O beware. . . . of jealousy;
It is the green-eyed monster which doth mock
The meat it feeds on.
Ibid.

Then must you speak

.   .   .   .

Of one not easily jealous, but being wrought
Perplex'd in the extreme.

Act V. Sc. 2.

Then a soldier,
Full of strange oaths and bearded like the pard,
Jealous in honour.

As You Like It.   Act II. Sc. 7.

God be praised for my jealousy!
Merry Wives of Windsor.   Act II. Sc. 2.

So full of artless jealousy is guilt,
It spills itself in fearing to be spilt.
Hamlet.   Act IV. Sc. 5.

O, how hast thou with jealousy infected
The sweetness of affiance!
King Henry V.   Act II. Sc. 2.

Self-harming jealousy! fie, beat it hence!
The Comedy of Errors.   Act II. Sc. 1.

How many fond fools serve mad jealousy!
Ibid.

And shuddering fear, and green-eyed jealousy!
The Merchant of Venice.   Act III. Sc. 2.

JUDGMENT

O judgment! thou art fled to brutish beasts,
And men have lost their reason.
Julius Cæsar.   Act III. Sc. 2.

Take our good meaning, for our judgment sits
Five times in that ere once in our five wits.
Romeo and Juliet.   Act I. Sc. 4.

How would you be
If He, which is the top of judgment, should
But judge you as you are?
Measure for Measure.   Act II. Sc. 2.

My salad days
When I was green in judgment.
Antony and Cleopatra.   Act I. Sc. 5

Men's judgments are
A parcel of their fortunes.
Act III. Sc. 11.

For what he has he gives, what thinks he shows;
Yet gives he not till judgment guides his bounty.
Troilus and Cressida.   Act IV. Sc. 5.

I have, perhaps, some shallow spirit of judgment.
King Henry VI.   Part I.   Act II. Sc. 4.

If my suspect be false, forgive me, God,
For judgment only doth belong to thee.
Part II.   Act III. Sc. 2

JUSTICE

This even-handed justice
Commends the ingredients of our poison'd chalice
To our own lips.

Macbeth. Act I. Sc. 7.

Tremble, thou wretch,
That hast within thee undivulged crimes,
Unwhipp'd of justice.

King Lear. Act III. Sc. 2.

See how yond justice rails upon yond simple
thief.

Act IV. Sc. 6.

Therefore, Jew,
Though justice be thy plea, consider this,
That, in the course of justice, none of us
Should see salvation.

The Merchant of Venice. Act IV. Sc. 1.

JESTS

You break jests as braggarts do their blades
which . . . hurt not.

Much Ado About Nothing. Act V. Sc. 1.

O jest unseen, inscrutable, invisible,
As a nose on a man's face, or a weathercock on a
steeple!

The Two Gentlemen of Verona. Act II. Sc. 1.

A jest's prosperity lies in the ear
Of him that hears it, never in the tongue
Of him that makes it.

Love's Labour's Lost.   Act V. Sc. 2.

If you will jest with me, know my aspect
And fashion your demeanor to my looks.

Comedy of Errors.   Act II. Sc. 2.

His jest will savour but of shallow wit,
When thousands weep more than did laugh at it.

King Henry V.   Act I. Sc. 2.

He jests at scars that never felt a wound.

Romeo and Juliet.   Act II. Sc. 2.

KING

I'll call thee Hamlet,
King, father, royal Dane.

Hamlet.   Act I. Sc. 4.

The play's the thing
Wherein I'll catch the conscience of the king.

Act II. Sc. 2.

A king of shreds and patches.

Act III. Sc. 4.

A mockery king of snow.

King Richard II.   Act IV. Sc. 1.

If he be not fellow with the best king, thou
shalt find the best king of good fellows.

King Henry V.   Act V. Sc. 2.

Ay, every inch a king.

King Lear.   Act IV. Sc. 6.

LOVE

In the sweetest bud
The eating canker dwells; so eating love
Inhabits in the finest wits of all.

The Two Gentlemen of Verona.   Act I. Sc. 1.

Even so by love the young and tender wit
Is turned to folly.

Ibid.

Jul.   They do not love that do not show their love.
Luc.   O, they love least that let men know their
love!

Sc. 2.

O, how this spring of love resembleth
The uncertain glory of an April day!

Sc. 3.

Love is blind.

Act II. Sc. 1.

Though the chameleon Love can feed on the air,
I am one that am nourished by my victuals.

Ibid.

(*Val.*)   Love hath twenty pair of eyes.
Sc. 4.

(*Thu.*)   They say that love hath not an eye at all.
Ibid.

Love hath chased sleep from my enthralled eyes
And made them watchers of mine own heart's
sorrow.
The Two Gentlemen of Verona.   Act II. Sc. 4.

Love 's a mighty lord.
Ibid.

For love, thou know'st, is full of jealousy!
Ibid.

Love bade me swear and Love bids me forswear.
O, sweet suggesting Love!
Sc. 6.

Didst thou but know the inly touch of love,
Thou wouldst as soon go kindle fire with snow
As seek to quench the fire of love with words.
Sc. 7.

For Love is like a child,
That longs for everything that he can come by.
Act III. Sc. 1.

Yet, spaniel-like, the more she spurns my love,
The more it grows and fawneth on her still.
Act IV. Sc. 2.

But love will not be spurr'd to what it loathes.
Two Gentlemen of Verona. Act V. Sc. 1.

O, 'tis the curse in love, and still approved,
When women cannot love where they're beloved!
Sc. 4.

The course of true love never did run smooth.
Midsummer Night's Dream. Act I. Sc. 1.

O, then, what graces in my love do dwell,
That he hath turn'd a heaven unto a hell!
Ibid.

Things base and vile, holding no quantity,
Love can transpose to form and dignity.
Ibid.

Love looks not with the eyes, but with the mind;
And therefore is wing'd Cupid painted blind.
Ibid.

And therefore is Love said to be a child,
Because in choice he is so oft beguiled.
Ibid.

As waggish boys in games themselves forswear,
So the boy love is perjured everywhere.
Ibid.

Love, therefore, and tongue-tied simplicity
In least speak most, to my capacity.
Act V. Sc. 1.

But love is blind and lovers can not see
'The pretty follies that themselves commit.
>> The Merchant of Venice.   Act II. Sc. 6.

Love is merely a madness, and . . . . deserves
as well a dark house and a whip as madmen do.
>> As You Like It.   Act III. Sc. 2.

Love's tongue proves dainty Bacchus gross in
taste:
For valour, is not love a Hercules?
>> Love's Labour's Lost.   Act. IV. Sc. 3.

And when Love speaks, the voice of all the gods
Make heaven drowsy with the harmony.
>> Ibid.

In love the heavens themselves do guide the
state;
Money buys lands, and wives are sold by fate.
>> The Merry Wives of Windsor.   Act V. Sc. 5.

Love-thoughts lie rich when canopied with
bowers.
>> Twelfth Night.   Act I. Sc. 1.

Love sought is good, but given unsought is
better.
>> Act III. Sc. 1.

She never told her love,
But let concealment, like a worm i' the bud,
Feed on her damask cheek.
>> Twelfth Night.   Act II. Sc. 4.

If love be blind, love can not hit the mark.

Romeo and Juliet. Act II. Sc. 1.

Young men's love then lies
Not truly in their hearts, but in their eyes.

Sc. 3.

Love's heralds should be thoughts,
Which ten times faster glide than the sun's
beams.

Sc. 5.

Love's reason 's without reason.

Cymbeline. Act IV. Sc. 2.

Speak low, if you speak love.

Much Ado About Nothing. Act II. Sc. 1.

This is the very ecstasy of love.

Hamlet. Act II. Sc. 1.

The pangs of despised love.

Act III. Sc. 1.

What my love is, proof hath made you know;
And as my love is sized, my fear is so.

Sc. 2.

Where love is great the littlest doubts are fear;
Where little fears grow great, great love grows
there.

Ibid.

There's beggary in the love that can be reckon'd.

Antony and Cleopatra. Act I. Sc. 1.

LIFE

I do not set my life at a pin's fee.
Hamlet.   Act I. Sc. 4.

I can not tell what you and other men
Think of this life; but, for my single self,
I had as lief not be as live to be
In awe of such a thing as I myself.
Julius Cæsar.   Act I. Sc. 2.

I bear a charmed life.
Macbeth.   Act V. Sc. 8.

He hath a daily beauty in his life.
Othello.   Act V. Sc. 1.

And this our life, exempt from public haunt,
Finds tongues in trees, books in the running brooks,
Sermons in stones and good in everything.
As You Like It.   Act II. Sc. 1.

Think you I bear the shears of destiny?
Have I commandment on the pulse of life?
King John.   Act IV. Sc. 2.

That life is better life, past fearing death,
Than that which lives to fear.
Measure for Measure.   Act V. Sc. 1.

O, this life
Is nobler than attending for a check,
Prouder than rustling in unpaid-for silk.
Cymbeline   Act III. Sc. 3.

MAN

O, how wretched
Is that poor man that hangs on princes' favours!
King Henry VIII.   Act III. Sc. 2.

An old man, broken with the storms of state,
Is come to lay his weary bones among ye.
Act IV. Sc. 2.

This is a slight unmeritable man,
Meet to be sent on errands.
Julius Cæsar.   Act IV. Sc. 1.

There's many a man hath more hair than wit.
Comedy of Errors.   Act II. Sc. 2.

I am a woman's man and besides myself.
Act. III. Sc. 2.

A man of my kidney.
Merry Wives of Windsor.   Act III. Sc. 5.

I am a man
More sinn'd against than sinning.
King Lear.   Act III. Sc. 2.

He can not be a perfect man,
Not being tried and tutor'd in the world.
The Two Gentlemen of Verona.   Act I. Sc. 3.

A man I am cross'd with adversity.
Act IV. Sc. 1.

O heaven! were man
But constant, he were perfect.

Act V. Sc. 4.

Give every man thy ear, but few thy voice.

Hamlet.   Act I. Sc. 3.

Take each man's censure, but reserve thy judgment.

Ibid.

Give me that man
That is not passion's slave.

Act III. Sc. 2.

What is a man
If his chief good and market of his time
Be but to sleep and feed?

Act IV. Sc. 4.

MEN

Men's evil manners live in brass; their virtues
We write in water.

King Henry VIII.   Act IV. Sc. 2.

But we are all men,
In our own natures frail, and capable
Of our flesh; few are angels.

Act V. Sc. 3.

Men at some time are masters of their fates.

Julius Cæsar.   Act I. Sc. 2.

Let me have men about me that are fat;
Sleek-headed men and such as sleep o' nights.
Ibid.

The evil that men do lives after them;
The good is oft interred with their bones.
Act III. Sc. 2.

They say, best men are moulded out of faults.
Measure for Measure.   Act V. Sc. 1.

O, what men dare do! what men may do! what
men daily do, not knowing what they do!
Much Ado About Nothing.   Act IV. Sc. 1.

Men's vows are women's traitors!
Cymbeline.   Act III. Sc. 4.

O, give me the spare men and spare me the great
    ones.
King Henry IV.   Part II.   Act III. Sc. 2.

MERCY

Mercy is not itself that oft looks so.
Measure for Measure.   Act II. Sc. 1.

No ceremony that to great ones 'longs   .   .   .
Becomes them with one-half so good a grace
As mercy does.
Sc. 2.

Lawful mercy
Is nothing kin to foul redemption.

Sc. 4.

Sweet mercy is nobility's true badge.
Titus Andronicus.   Act I. Sc. 1.

The quality of mercy is not strain'd,
It droppeth as the gentle rain from heaven
Upon the place beneath.
The Merchant of Venice.   Act IV. Sc. 1.

But mercy is above this sceptred sway.
Ibid

And earthly power doth then show likest God's
When mercy seasons justice.
Ibid.

We do pray for mercy;
And that same prayer doth teach us all to render
The deeds of mercy.
Ibid.

The gates of mercy shall be all shut up.
King Henry V.   Act III. Sc. 3.

MUSIC

Makes a swan-like end,
Fading in music.

Merchant of Venice. Act III. Sc. 2.

Here will we sit and let the sounds of music creep
in our ears.

Act V. Sc. 1.

The man that hath no music in himself,
Nor is not moved with concord of sweet sounds,
Is fit for treasons, stratagems and spoils: . . .
Let no such man be trusted.

Ibid.

It will discourse most eloquent music.

Hamlet. Act III. Sc. 2.

If music be the food of love, play on.

Twelfth Night. Act I. Sc. 1.

I had rather hear you to solicit that
Than music from the spheres.

Act III. Sc. 2.

In sweet music is such art,
Killing care and grief of heart,
Fall asleep, or hearing, die.

King Henry VIII. Song. Act III. Sc. 1.

Tax not so bad a voice
To slander music any more than once.

Much Ado About Nothing. Act II. Sc. 3.

Wilt thou have music? hark! Apollo plays
And twenty caged nightingales do sing.
>> Taming of the Shrew. Induction. Sc. 2.

One whom the music of his own vain tongue
Doth ravish like enchanting harmony.
>> Love's Labour's Lost. Act I. Sc. 1.

The music of the spheres!
>> Pericles. Act V. Sc. 1.

MADNESS

I am but mad north-north-west; when the wind is
southerly I know a hawk from a handsaw.
>> Hamlet. Act II. Sc. 2.

Though this be madness, yet there is method
in ''
>> Ibid.

Mad call I it; for, to define true madness,
What is 't but to be nothing else but mad?
>> Ibid.

That he is mad 'tis true; 'tis true, 'tis pity;
And pity 'tis, 'tis true.
>> Ibid.

Madness in great ones must not unwatched go.
Act III. Sc. 1.

If she be mad,—as I believe, no other,—
Her madness hath the oddest frame of sense.
Measure for Measure.   Act V. Sc. 1.

Good Lord, what madness rules in brain-sick men!
King Henry VI.   Part I.   Act IV. Sc. 1.

This is very midsummer madness.
Twelfth Night.   Act III. Sc. 4.

Mad world! mad kings! mad composition!
King John.   Act II. Sc. 1.

I am not mad; I would to heaven I were!
Act III. Sc. 4.

I am not mad; too well, too well I feel
The different plague of each calamity.
Ibid.

Thou art essentially mad, without seeming so.
King Henry IV. Act II. Sc. 4.

O, that way madness lies; let me shun that.
King Lear.   Act III. Sc. 4.

NAME

Your name is great
In mouths of wisest censure.
Othello.   Act II. Sc. 3.

Good name in man and woman   .   .   .
Is the immediate jewel of their souls.
Act III. Sc. 3.

But he that filches from me my good name
Robs me of that which not enriches him
And makes me poor indeed.
Ibid.

What's in a name? that which we call a rose
By any other name would smell as sweet.
Romeo and Juliet.   Act II. Sc. 2.

Frailty, thy name is woman !
Hamlet.   Act I. Sc. 2.

I can not tell what the dickens his name is.
The Merry Wives of Windsor.   Act III. Sc. 2.

OFFENCE

Hence hath offence his quick celerity,
When it is borne in high authority.
Measure for Measure.   Act IV. Sc. 2.

O, my offence is rank, it smells to heaven.
Hamlet.   Act III. Sc. 3.

In the corrupted currents of this world
Offence's gilded hand may shove by justice.
Ibid.

And where the offence is let the great axe fall.
Act. IV. Sc. 5.

All 's not offence that indiscretion finds
And dotage terms so.
King Lear. Act II. Sc. 4.

OBSERVATION

He is a great observer, and he looks
Quite through the deeds of men.
Julius Cæsar. Act I. Sc. 2.

The observed of all observers.
Hamlet. Act III. Sc. 1.

By my penny of observation.
Love's Labour's Lost. Act III. Sc. 1.

What observation madest thou in this case
Of his heart's meteors tilting in his face?
The Comedy of Errors. Act IV. Sc. 2.

For he is but a bastard to the time
That doth not smack of observation.
King John. Act I. Sc. 1.

He hath strange places cramm'd with observation.
As You Like It. Act II. Sc. 7.

PRAYER

Being thus frighted swears a prayer or two,
And sleeps again.
Romeo and Juliet.   Act I. Sc. 4.

Nor tears nor prayers shall purchase out abuses.
Act III. Sc. 1.

He prays but faintly and would be denied;
We pray with heart and soul and all beside.
King Richard II.   Act V. Sc. 3.

His prayers are full of false hypocrisy;
Ours of true zeal and deep integrity.
Ibid.

Our prayers do out-pray his; then let them have
That mercy which true prayer ought to have.
Ibid.

He scorns to say his prayers, lest a' should be
thought a coward.
King Henry V.   Act III. Sc. 2.

And what's in prayer but this two-fold force,
To be forestalled ere we come to fall,
Or pardon'd being down?
Hamlet.   Act III. Sc. 3.

With true prayers
That shall be up at heaven and enter there
Ere sun-rise, prayers from preserved souls.
Measure for Measure.   Act II. Sc. 2.

When I would pray and think, I think and pray
To several subjects.

Sc. 4.

Truly . . . I would desire you to clap into
your prayers.

Act IV. Sc. 3.

And my ending is despair,
Unless I be relieved by prayer,
Which pierces so that it assaults
Mercy itself and frees all faults.

The Tempest Epilogue.

The more my prayer, the lesser is my grace.

Midsummer Night's Dream.   Act II. Sc. 2.

If when you make your prayers,
God should be so obdurate as yourselves,
How would it fare with your departed souls?

King Henry VI.   Part II.   Act IV. Sc. 7.

I have said my prayers and devil Envy say Amen.

Troilus and Cressida.   Act II. Sc. 3.

If I could pray to move prayers would move me.

Julius Cæsar.   Act III. Sc. 1.

When thou hast leisure say thy prayers.

All's Well That Ends Well.   Act I. Sc. 1.

PATIENCE

She sat like patience on a monument
Smiling at grief.

> Twelfth Night.   Act II. Sc. 4.

I thank God I have as little patience as another
man.

> Love's Labour's Lost.   Act I. Sc. 2.

For a very little thief of occasion will rob you of
a great deal of patience.

> Coriolanus.   Act II. Sc. 1.

That which in mean men we entitle patience
Is pale cowardice in noble breasts.

> King Richard II.   Act I. Sc. 2.

Patience is stale, and I am weary of it.

> Act V. Sc. 5.

Though patience be a tired mare, yet she will
plod.

> King Henry V.   Act II. Sc. 1.

O, you blessed ministers above,
Keep me in patience!

> Measure for Measure.   Act V. Sc. 1.

How poor are they that have not patience!

> Othello.   Act II. Sc. 3.

Patience, thou young and rose-lipp'd cherubin.

> Act IV. Sc. 2.

Here will be an old abusing of God's patience
and the king's English.
The Merry Wives of Windsor. Act I. Sc. 4.

Patience and sorrow strove
Who should express her goodliest.
King Lear. Act IV. Sc. 3.

'Tis all men's office to speak patience
To those that wring under the load of sorrow.
Much Ado About Nothing. Act V. Sc. 1.

PEACE

In peace there's nothing so becomes a man
As modest stillness and humility.
King Henry V. Act III. Sc. 1.

Who should study to prefer a peace,
If holy churchmen take delight in broils?
King Henry VI. Part I. Act III. Sc. 1.

Why, I, in this weak piping time of peace,
Have no delight to pass away the time.
King Richard III. Act I. Sc. 1.

Still in thy right hand carry gentle peace,
To silence envious tongues.
King Henry VIII. Act III. Sc. 2.

He gave his honours to the world again,
His blessed part to heaven, and slept in peace.
Act IV. Sc. 2

The peace of heaven is theirs that lift their
  swords
In such a just and charitable war.
King John.   Act II. Sc. 1.

        And on the marriage-bed
Of smiling peace to march a bloody host,
And make a riot on the gentle brow
Of true sincerity?
Act III. Sc. 1.

In war was never lion raged more fierce,
In peace was never gentle lamb more mild.
King Richard II.   Act II. Sc. 1.

The cankers of a calm world and a long peace.
King Henry IV.   Part I.   Act IV. Sc. 2.

I speak of peace, while covert enmity
Under the smile of safety wounds the world.
Part II.   Induction.

Out of the speech of peace that bears such grace,
Into the harsh and boisterous tongue of war?
Act IV. Sc. 1.

Our peace will, like a broken limb united,
Grow stronger for the breaking.
Ibid.

PITY

Forget to pity him, lest thy pity prove
A serpent that will sting thee to the heart.
King Richard II.   Act V. Sc. 3.

He hath a tear for pity and a hand
Open as day for meeting charity.
King Henry IV.   Part II.   Act IV. Sc. 4.

Pity was all the fault that was in me.
King Henry VI.   Part II.   Act III. Sc. 1.

O, pity, pity, gentle heaven, pity!
Part III.   Act II. Sc. 5.

But yet the pity of it, Iago!
O Iago, the pity of it, Iago!
Othello.   Act IV. Sc. 1.

And wiped our eyes
Of drops that sacred pity hath engender'd.
As You Like It.   Act II. Sc. 7.

Is there no pity sitting in the clouds,
That sees into the bottom of my grief?
Romeo and Juliet.   Act III. Sc. 5.

PHILOSOPHY

There are more things in heaven and earth, Horatio,
Than are dreamt of in your philosophy.
Hamlet.   Act I. Sc. 5.

There is something in this more than natural, if philosophy could find it out.
Act II. Sc. 2.

To love, to wealth, to pomp, I pine and die;
With all these living in philosophy.
Love's Labour's Lost.   Act I. Sc. 1.

Of your philosophy you make no use,
If you give place to accidental evils.
Julius Cæsar.   Act IV. Sc. 3.

Adversity's sweet milk, philosophy.
Romeo and Juliet.   Act III. Sc. 3.

For there was never yet philosopher
That could endure the toothache patiently.
Much Ado About Nothing.   Act V. Sc. 1.

I am . . . . . .
Glad that you thus continue your resolve
To suck the sweets of sweet philosophy.
Taming of the Shrew.   Act I. Sc. 1.

QUARREL

Beware
Of entrance to a quarrel, but being in,
Bear 't that the opposed may beware of thee.
Hamlet. Act I. Sc. 3.

But greatly to find quarrel in a straw
When honour 's at the stake.
Act IV. Sc. 4.

Thrice is he armed that hath his quarrel just.
King Henry VI. Part II. Act III. Sc. 2.

Sudden and quick in quarrel.
As You Like It. Act II. Sc. 7.

O . . . we quarrel in print, by the book;
as you have books for good manners.
As You Like It. Act V. Sc. 4.

Thy head is as full of quarrels as an egg is full
of meat.
Romeo and Juliet. Act III. Sc. 1.

In a false quarrel there is no true valour.
Much Ado About Nothing. Act V. Sc. 1.

REMEDY

Things without all remedy
Should be without regard.
Macbeth.   Act III. Sc. 2.

And He that might the vantage best have took
Found out the remedy.
Measure for Measure.   Act II. Sc. 2.

I can get no remedy against this consumption of
the purse.
King Henry IV.   Part II.   Act I. Sc. 2.

When remedies are past, the griefs are ended
By seeing the worst, which late on hopes depended.
Othello.   Act I. Sc. 3.

Our remedies oft in ourselves do lie,
Which we ascribe to heaven.
All's Well That Ends Well.   Act I. Sc. 1.

REASON

Neither rhyme nor reason can express how much.
As You Like It.   Act III. Sc. 2.

The will of man is by his reason sway'd.
Midsummer Night's Dream.   Act II. Sc. 2.

Reason becomes the marshal to my will.
Ibid.

To say the truth, reason and love keep little company together nowadays.

Act III. Sc. 1.

Reason thus with life :

If I do lose thee, I do lose a thing
That none but fools would keep.

Measure for Measure.   Act III. Sc. 1.

Now, see that noble and most sovereign reason,
Like sweet bells jangled, out of tune and harsh.

Hamlet.   Act III. Sc. 1.

· SOUL

O my prophetic soul !

Hamlet.   Act I. Sc. 5.

Since my dear soul was mistress of her choice,
And could of men distinguish, her election
Hath seal'd thee for herself.

Act III. Sc. 2.

O, it offends me to the soul to hear a robustious periwig-pated fellow tear a passion to tatters.

Ibid

O limed soul, that, struggling to be free,
Art more engaged !

Sc. 3.

Lay not that flattering unction to your soul.

Act III. Sc. 4.

My soul is full of discord and dismay.
                                        Act IV. Sc. 1

To my sick soul, as sin's true nature is,
Each toy seems prologue to some great amiss.
                                        Sc. 5.

I have a kind soul that would give you thanks
And knows not how to do it but with tears.
                            King John.   Act V. Sc. 7.

Now my soul hath elbow-room.
                                        Ibid.

And from the organ-pipe of frailty sings
His soul and body to their lasting rest.
                                        Ibid.

Plain well-meaning soul,
Whom fair befal in heaven 'mongst happy souls!
                        King Richard II.   Act II. Sec. 1.

Now hast my soul brought forth her prodigy.
                                        Sec. 2.

An evil soul producing holy witness
Is like a villain with a smiling cheek.
                    The Merchant of Venice.   Act I. Sc. 3.

A wretched soul, bruised with adversity.
                    The Comedy of Errors.   Act II. Sc. 1.

All the souls that were were forfeit once.
                    Measure for Measure.   Act II. Sc. 2.

The soul of this man is his clothes.
All's Well That Ends Well. . Act II. Sc. 5.

I have a soul of lead
So stakes me to the ground I can not move.
Romeo and Juliet.   Act I. Sc. 4.

I will deal in this
As secretly and justly as your soul
Should with your body.
Much Ado About Nothing.   Act IV. Sc. 1.

SORROW

O, if thou teach me to believe this sorrow,
Teach thou this sorrow how to make me die.
King John.   Act III. Sc. 1.

I will instruct my sorrows to be proud.
Ibid.

Here I and sorrows sit.
Ibid.

But now will canker sorrow eat my bud
And chase the native beauty from his cheek.
Sc. 4.

To seek out sorrow that dwells everywhere.
King Richard II.   Act I. Sc. 2.

For gnarling sorrow hath less power to bite
The man that mocks at it and sets it light.

Sc. 3.

Fell sorrow's tooth doth never rankle more
Than when he bites, but lanceth not the sore.

Ibid.

Give sorrow leave awhile to tutor me
To this submission.

Act IV. Sc. 1.

One sorrow never comes but brings an heir.

Pericles.   Act I. Sc. 4.

When sorrows come, they come not single spies,
But in battalions.

Hamlet.   Act IV. Sc. 5.

Are you like the painting of a sorrow,
A face without a heart?

Sc. 7.

Sorrow would be a rarity most beloved,
If all could so become it.

King Lear.   Act IV. Sc. 3.

Affliction may one day smile again; and till then,
Sit thee down, sorrow.

Love's Labour's Lost.   Act I. Sc. 1.

And sleep, that sometimes shuts up sorrow's eye,
Steal me awhile from mine own company.

Midsummer Night's Dream.   Act III Sc. 2.

But sorrow, that is couch'd in seeming gladness,
Is like that mirth fate turns to sudden sadness.
Troilus and Cresseda. Act I. Sc. 1.

Sorrow concealed, like an oven stopp'd,
Doth burn the heart to cinders where it is.
Titus Andronicus. Act II. Sc. 4.

Is not my sorrow deep, having no bottom?
Act III. Sc. 1.

SLEEP

O sleep, thou ape of death, lie dull upon her!
Cymbeline. Act II. Sc. 2.

He that sleeps feels not the toothache.
Act V. Sc. 4.

Sleep shall neither night nor day
Hang upon his pent-house lid.
Macbeth. Act I. Sc. 3.

The innocent sleep,
Sleep that knits up the ravell'd sleave of care.
Act II. Sc. 2.

O sleep, O gentle sleep,
Nature's soft nurse !
King Henry IV. Part II. Act III. Sc. 1.

SAINT

And seem a saint, when most I play the devil.
King Richard III.   Act I. Sc. 3.

O, thou hast damnable iteration, and art indeed
able to corrupt a saint.
King Henry IV.   Part I.   Act I. Sc. 2.

I hold you as a thing ensky'd, and sainted . . . .
And to be talk'd with in sincerity,
As with a saint.
Measure for Measure.   Act I. Sc. 5.

I conjure thee by all the saints in heaven !
The Comedy of Errors.   Act IV. Sc. 4.

SIN

Some sins do bear their privilege on earth.
King John.   Act I. Sc. 1.

'Tis no sin for a man to labour in his vocation.
King Henry IV.   Part I.   Act I. Sc. 2.

If to be old and merry be a sin, then many an old
host that I know is damned.
King Henry IV.   Part I.   Act II. Sc. 4.

Commit
The oldest sins the newest kind of ways?
Part II.   Act IV. Sc. 5.

Self-love . . is not so vile a sin
As self-neglecting.
King Henry V. Act II. Sc. 4.

But if it be a sin to covet honour,
I am the most offending soul alive.
Act IV. Sc. 3.

It is a great sin to swear unto a sin,
But greater sin to keep a sinful oath.
King Henry VI. Part II. Act V. Sc. 1.

But I am in
So far in blood that sin will pluck on sin.
King Richard III. Act IV. Sc. 2.

But cardinal sins and hollow hearts I fear ye.
King Henry VIII. Act III. Sc. 1.

By that sin fell the angels.
Sc. 2.

Some rise by sin, and some by virtue fall.
Measure for Measure. Act II. Sc. 1.

Our compell'd sins
Stand more for number than for accompt.
Sc. 4.

Nothing emboldens sin so much as mercy.
Timon of Athens. Act III. Sc. 5.

You can not make gross sins look clear.
Ibid.

The sin of my ingratitude even now
Was heavy on me.

Macbeth. Act I. Sc. 4.

Teach sin the carriage of a holy saint.

Comedy of Errors. Act III. Sc. 1.

Cut off even in the blossoms of my sin.

Hamlet. Act I. Sc. 5.

Few love to hear the sins they love to act.

Pericles. Act I. Sc. 1.

For he's no man on whom perfections wait
That, knowing sin within, will touch the gate.

Ibid.

One sin, I know, another doth provoke.

Ibid.

When devils will the blackest sins put on,
They do suggest at first with heavenly shows.

Othello. Act II. Sc. 3.

O, what authority and show of truth
Can cunning sin cover itself withal!

Much Ado About Nothing. Act IV. Sc. 1.

SLANDER

Only his gift is in devising impossible slanders.
          Much Ado About Nothing.   Act II. Sc. 1.

Thy slander hath gone through and through her
heart.
                                        Act V. Sc. 1.

Slander'd to death by villains.
                                        Ibid.

Betrays to slander,
Whose sting is sharper than the sword's.
               The Winter's Tale.   Act II. Sc. 3.

No, 'tis slander,
Whose edge is sharper than the sword, whose
tongue
Outvenoms all the worms of Nile.
                    Cymbeline.   Act III. Sc. 4.

For slander lives upon succession,
Forever housed where it gets possession.
          The Comedy of Errors.   Act. III. Sc. 1.

That is no slander which is a truth.
               Romeo and Juliet.   Act IV. Sc. 1.

There is no slander in an allowed fool, though
he do nothing but rail.
                    Twelfth Night.   Act I. Sc. 5.

A partial slander sought I to avoid,
And in the sentence my own life destroy'd.
                    King Richard II.   Act I. Sc. 3.

TONGUE

He speaks plain cannon fire, and smoke, and
    bounce;
He gives the bastinado with his tongue.
King John.   Act. II. Sc. 1.

O, that my tongue were in the thunder's mouth!
Act III. Sc. 4.

My tongue shall hush again this storm of war
And make fair weather in your blustering land.
Act V. Sc. 2.

Let the tongue of war
Plead for our interest and our being here.
Ibid.

O, but they say the tongues of dying men
Enforce attention like deep harmony.
King Richard II.   Act II. Sc. 1.

He does me double wrong
That wounds me with the flatteries of his tongue.
Act III. Sc. 2.

My tongue could never learn sweet smoothing
    words.
King Richard III.   Act I. Sc. 2

Every tongue brings in a several tale,
And every tale condemns me for a villain.
Act V. Sc. 3.

How silver-sweet sound lovers' tongues by night,
Like softest music to attending ears !
Romeo and Juliet. Act II. Sc. 2.

That man that hath a tongue, I say, is no man,
If with his tongue he can not win a woman.
The Two Gentlemen of Verona. Act III. Sc. 1.

While thou livest, keep a good tongue in thy
head.
The Tempest. Act III. Sc. 2.

The Iron tongue of midnight hath told twelve.
The Midsummer Night's Dream. Act V. Sc. 1.

No, let the candied tongue lick absurd pomp,
And crook the pregnant hinges of the knee
Where thrift may follow fawning.
Hamlet. Act III. Sc. 2.

L. of C.

Put a tongue
In every wound of Cæsar that should move
The stones of Rome to rise and mutiny.
Julius Cæsar. Act III. Sc. 2.

TIME

But here, upon this bank and shoal o' time,
We 'ld jump the life to come.
Macbeth. Act I. Sc. 7.

Live to be the show and gaze o' the time.
Act V. Sc. 8.

Time is a very bankrupt, and owes more than
he 's worth to season.

The Comedy of Errors.   Act IV. Sc. 3.

Have you not heard men say,
That Time comes stealing on by night and day?

Ibid.

If Time be in debt and theft, and a sergeant in
the way,
Hath he not reason to turn back an hour in a
day?

Ibid.

The end crowns all,
And that old common arbitrator, Time,
Will one day end it.

Troilus and Cressida.   Act IV. Sc. 5.

Old Time, the clock-setter, that bald sexton, Time,
Is it as he will?

King John.   Act III. Sc. 1.

O, call back yesterday, bid time return!

King Richard II.   Act III. Sc. 2.

Time shall unfold what plaited cunning hides.

King Lear.   Act I. Sc. 1.

The time is out of joint; O cursed spite,
That ever I was born to set it right!

Hamlet.   Act I. Sc. 5.

What seest thou else
In the dark backward and abyss of time?
The Tempest.   Act I. Sc. 2.

The inaudible and noiseless foot of time.
All's Well That Ends Well.   Act V. Sc. 3.

Time and the hour runs through the roughest
day.
Macbeth.   Act I. Sc. 3.

To beguile the time,
Look like the time; bear welcome in your eye,
Your hand, your tongue.
Sc. 5.

USES

How weary, stale, flat and unprofitable,
Seem to me all the uses of this world!
Hamlet.   Act I. Sc. 2.

For use almost can change the stamp of nature.
Act III. Sc. 4.

To what base uses we may return!
Act V. Sc. 1.

How use doth breed a habit in a man!
The Two Gentlemen of Verona.   Act V. Sc. 4.

Sweet are the uses of adversity.
As You Like It.   Act II. Sc. 1.

VIRTUE

I see virtue in his looks.
King Henry IV. Part I. Act II. Sc. 4.

Is there no virtue extant?
Ibid.

Virtue is not regarded in handicrafts-men.
King Henry VI. Part II. Act IV. Sc. 2.

Her virtues graced with external gifts
Do breed love's settled passions in my heart.
Act. V. Sc. 5.

Virtue itself 'scapes not calumnious strokes.
Hamlet. Act I. Sc. 3.

But virtue, as it never will be moved,
Though lewdness court it in a shape of heaven.
Sc. 5.

Assume a virtue, if you have it not.
Act III. Sc. 4.

Virtue itself of vice must beg pardon.
Ibid.

Virtue itself turns vice, being misapplied,
And vice sometimes by action dignified.
Romeo and Juliet. Act II. Sc. 3.

If our virtues
Did not go forth of us, 'twere all alike
As if we had them not.
Measure for Measure. Act I. Sc. 1.

Virtue is bold, and goodness never fearful.
Act III. Sc. 1.

Make a virtue of necessity.
Two Gentlemen of Verona. Act IV. Sc. 1.

The rarer action is
In virtue than in vengeance.
The Tempest. Act V. Sc. 1.

You nickname virtue . . .
For virtue's office never breaks men's troth.
Love's Labour's Lost. Act V. Sc. 2.

Virtue is beauty, but the beauteous evil
Are empty trunks o'erflourished with the devil.
Twelfth Night. Act III. Sc. 4.

My heart laments that virtue can not live
Out of the teeth of emulation.
Julius Cæsar. Act II. Sc. 3.

So our virtues
Lie in the interpretation of the time.
Coriolanus. Act IV. Sc. 7.

Can virtue hide itself?
Much Ado About Nothing. Act II. Sc. 1.

VILLAIN

O villain! thou wilt be condemned into everlasting redemption for this.
> Much Ado About Nothing. Act IV. Sc. 2.

Villain and he be many miles asunder.
> Romeo and Juliet. Act III. Sc. 5.

O villain, villain, smiling, damned villain!
> Hamlet. Act I. Sc. 5.

My tables,—meet it is I set it down,
That one may smile, and smile, and be a villain.
> Ibid.

As if we were villains by necessity; fools by heavenly compulsion.
> King Lear. Act I. Sc. 2.

Though I can not be said to be a flattering honest man, it must not be denied but I am a plain-dealing villain.
> Much Ado About Nothing. Act I. Sc. 3.

Precise villains they are, that I am sure of; and void of all profanation in the world that good Christians ought to have.
> Measure for Measure. Act II. Sc. 1.

Thou wert better thou hadst struck thy mother, thou paper-faced villain.
> King Henry IV. Part II. Act V. Sc. 4.

The villainy you teach me, I will execute, and it shall go hard but I will better the instruction.

The Merchant of Venice. Act III. Sc. 1.

WOMAN

A poor lone woman.

King Henry IV. Part II. Act II. Sc. 1,

These women are shrewd tempters with their tongues.

King Henry VI. Part I. Act I. Sc. 2.

O most pernicious woman!

Hamlet. Act I. Sc. 5.

How hard it is for women to keep counsel!

Julius Cæsar. Act II. Sc. 4.

Would it not grieve a woman to be overmastered with a piece of valiant dust? to make an account of her life to a clod of wayward marl?

Much Ado About Nothing. Act II. Sc. 1.

Let not women's weapons, water-drops,
Stain my man's cheeks!

King Lear. Act II. Sc. 4.

I have no other but a woman's reason;
I think him so because I think him so.

The Two Gentlemen of Verona. Act I. Sc. 2.

O, that she could speak now like a wood woman!

Act II. Sc. 3.

A woman sometimes scorns what best contents her.

Act III. Sc. 1.

The venom clamours of a jealous woman
Poisons more deadly than a mad dog's tooth.

The Comedy of Errors.   Act V. Sc. 1.

For where is any author in the world
Teaches such beauty as a woman's eye?

Love's Labour's Lost.   Act IV. Sc. 3.

She is a woman, therefore may be woo'd;
She is a woman, therefore may be won.

Titus Andronicus.   Act II. Sc. 1.

A woman moved is like a fountain troubled.

The Taming of the Shrew.   Act V. Sc. 2.

A woman would run through fire and water for such a kind heart.

Merry Wives of Windsor.   Act III. Sc. 4.

WORLD

Hereafter, in a better world than this,
I shall desire more love and knowledge of you.

As You Like It.   Act I. Sc. 2.

O, how full of briers is this working-day world!

Sc. 3.

O, what a world is this, when what is comely
Envenoms him that bears it!

Act II. Sc. 3.

You have too much respect upon the world;
They lose it that do buy it with much care.

The Merchant of Venice.   Act I. Sc. 1.

I hold the world but as the world   .   .   .
A stage where every man must play a part,
And mine a sad one.

Ibid.

The world is still deceived with ornament.

Act III. Sc. 2.

The world is not thy friend nor the world's law;
The world affords no law to make thee rich.

Romeo and Juliet.   Act V. Sc. 1.

An arrant traitor as any is in the universal world,
or in France, or in England!

King Henry V.   Act IV. Sc. 8.

Why, then the world's mine oyster,
Which I with sword will open.
The Merry Wives of Windsor. Act II. Sc. 2.

O world, how apt the poor are to be proud !
Twelfth Night. Act III. Sc. 1.

This world to me is like a lasting storm,
Whirring me from my friends.
Pericles. Act IV. Sc. 1.

O, let the vile world end,
And the promised flames of the last day
Knit earth and heaven together.
King Henry VI. Act V. Sc. 2.

It is a reeling world, indeed.
King Richard III. Act III. Sc. 2.

WORDS

My words fly up, my thoughts remain below:
Words without thoughts never to heaven go.
Hamlet. Act III. Sc. 3.

One doth not know
How much an ill word may empoison liking.
Much Ado About Nothing. Act III. Sc. 1.

Charm ache with air, and agony with words.
Act V. Sc. 1.

O, they have lived long on the alms-basket of words.

Love's Labour's Lost. Act V. Sc. 1.

Honest plain words best pierce the ear of grief.

Sc. 2.

But for your words, they rob the Hybla bees,
And leave them honeyless.

Julius Cæsar. Act V. Sc. 1.

A fine volley of words . . . . and quickly shot off.

The Two Gentlemen of Verona. Act II. Sc. 4.

You have an exchequer of words.

Ibid.

His words are bonds, his oaths are oracles,
His love sincere, his thoughts immaculate.

The Two Gentlemen of Verona. Act II. Sc. 7.

To be slow in words is a woman's only virtue.

Act III. Sc. 1.

Where words are scarce they are seldom spent
in vain,
For they breathe truth that breathe their words
in pain.

King Richard II. Act II. Sc. 1.

Zounds! I was never so bethumped with words
Since I first called my brother's father dad.

King John. Act II. Sc. 1.

They shoot but calm words folded up in smoke.

Ibid.

But words are words; I never yet did hear
That the bruised heart was pierced through the
ear.

Othello.   Act I. Sc. 3,

WAR

Now for the bare-picked bone of majesty
Doth dogged war bristle his angry crest.

King John.   Act IV. Sc. 3.

Away, and glister like the god of war.

Act V. Sc. 1.

He is come to open
The purple testament of bleeding war.

King Richard II.   Act III. Sc. 3.

But when the blast of war blows in our ears,
Then imitate the action of the tiger.

King Henry V.   Act III. Sc. 1.

The tyrant custom . . . .
Hath made the flinty and steel couch of war
My thrice-driven bed of down.

Othello.   Act I. Sc. 3.

O, wither'd is the garland of the war!

Antony and Cleopatra.   Act IV. Sc. 15.

Cry " havoc " and let slip the dogs of war.

Julius Cæsar.   Act III. Sc. 1.

WIT

I shall ne'er be ware of mine own wit till I break
my shins against it.

As You Like It.   Act II. Sc. 4.

Make the doors upon a woman's wit and it will
out at the casement.

Act IV. Sc. 1.

There's a skirmish of wit between them.

Much Ado About Nothing.   Act I. Sc. 1.

Thy wit is as quick as the greyhound's mouth.

Act V. Se. 2.

Devise, wit; write, pen.

Love's Labour's Lost.   Act I. Sc. 2.

That handful of wit!
Ah,   .   .   .   it is a most pathetical nit!

Act IV. Sc. 1.

He's winding up the watch of his wit; by and
by it will strike.

The Tempest.   Act II. Sc. 1.

When the age is in the wit is out.

Much Ado About Nothing.   Act III. Sc. 5.

A good wit will make use of anything.

King Henry IV.   Part II.   Act I. Sc. 2.

I am not only witty myself, but the cause that wit is in other men.

Ibid.

They have a plentiful lack of wit.

Hamlet. Act II. Sc. 1.

Upon her wit doth earthly honours wait,
And virtue stoops and trembles at her frown.

Titus Andronicus. Act II. Sc. 1.

YOUTH

We that are in the vaward of our youth.

King Henry IV. Part II. Act I. Sc. 2.

He was, indeed, the glass
Wherein the noble youth did dress themselves.

Act II. Sc. 3.

And in the morn and liquid dew of youth
Contagious blastments are most imminent.

Hamlet. Act I. Sc. 3.

He wears the rose
Of youth upon him.

Antony and Cleopatra. Act III. Sc. 13.

This morning, like the spirit of a youth
That means to be of note, begins betimes.
Act IV. Sc. 4.

We have some salt of our youth in us.
The Merry Wives of Windsor.   Act II. Sc. 3.

He that hath a beard is more than a youth, and he that hath no beard is less than a man.
Much Ado About Nothing.   Act II. Sc. 1.

Home-keeping youth have ever homely wits.
The Two Gentlemen of Verona.   Act I. Sc. 1.

MISCELLANEOUS.

A

Thus can the demigod Authority
Make us pay down for our offence by weight
The words of heaven.
                    Measure for Measure.   Act. I. Sc. 2.

What authority surfeits on would relieve us.
                    Coriolanus.   Act I. Sc. 1.

O, some authority how to proceed;
Some tricks, some quillets how to cheat the devil.
                    Love's Labour's Lost.   Act IV. Sc. 3.

Out of my lean and low ability
I'll lend you something.
                    Twelfth Night.   Act III. Sc. 4.

I dote on his very absence.
                    The Merchant of Venice.   Act I. Sc. 1.

A goodly apple rotten at the heart.
                                        Sc. 3.

Another lean unwashed artificer.
                    King John.   Act IV. Sc. 2.

Let me embrace thee, sour adversity,
For wise men say it is the wisest course.
                    King Henry VI.   Part III.   Act III. Sc. 2.

To dance attendance on their lordships' pleasures.
King Henry VIII.   Act V. Sc. 2.

Egregiously an ass.
Othello.   Act II. Sc. 1.

Smooth as monumental alabaster.
Act V. Sc. 2.

Season your admiration for a while.
Hamlet.   Act I. Sc. 2.

'Tis not so above;
There is no shuffling, there the action lies
In his true nature.
Act III. Sc. 3.

About some act that has no relish of salvation
in it.
Ibid.

Crabbed age and youth
Can not live together.
The Passionate Pilgrim, VIII.

All the perfumes of Arabia will not sweeten this
little hand.
Macbeth.   Act V. Sc. 1.

I could find it in my heart to disgrace my man's
apparel and to cry like a woman.
As You Like It.   Act II. Sc. 4.

The amity that wisdom knits not, folly may
easily untie.
Troilus and Cressida.   Act II. Sc. 3.

If for I want that glib and oily art,
To speak and purpose not.
King Lear.   Act I. Sc. 1.

Preposterous ass, that never read so far
To know the cause why music was ordained!
Taming of the Shrew.   Act III. Sc. 1.

B

Eating the bitter bread of banishment.
King Richard II.   Act III. Sc. 1.

But in the way of bargain, mark ye me,
I'll cavil on the ninth part of a hair.
King Henry IV.   Part I.   Act III. Sc. 1.

Once more unto the breach, dear friends, once
more.
King Henry V.   Act III. Sc. 1.

Gets him to rest cramm'd with distressful bread.
Act IV. Sc. 1.

'Tis better to be lowly born,
And range with humble livers in content,
Than to be perk'd up in a glistering grief,
And wear a golden sorrow.
King Henry VIII.   Act II. Sc. 3.

Beggar that I am, I am even poor in thanks,
Hamlet.   Act II. Sc. 2.

By and by is easily said.
Act III. Sc. 2.

A Cain-coloured beard.
Merry Wives of Windsor.   Act I. Sc. 4.

A beggarly account of empty boxes.
Romeo and Juliet.   Act V. Sc. 1.

Et tu, Brute!
Julius Cæsar.   Act III. Sc. 1.

I am in blood
Stepp'd in so far that, should I wade no more,
Returning were as tedious as go o'er.
Macbeth.   Act III. Sc. 4.

Shall I never see a bachelor of threescore again?
Much Ado About Nothing.   Act I. Sc. 1.

" In time the savage bull doth bear the yoke."
Ibid.

What need the bridge much broader than the flood?
Ibid.

I have for barbarism spoke more
Than for that angel knowledge you can say.
Love's Labour's Lost.   Act I. Sc. 1.

A very beadle to a humorous sigh.

Act III. Sc. 1.

Let me take you a button-hole lower.

Act V. Sc. 2.

The true beginning of our end.

A Midsummer Night's Dream.   Act V. Sc. 1.

'Tis not your inky brows, your black silk hair,
Your bugle eye-balls, nor your cheek of cream,
That can entame my spirits to your worship.

As You Like It.   Act III. Sc. 5.

Tell me what blessings I have here alive,
That I should fear to die?

The Winter's Tale.   Act III. Sc. 2.

We are born to do benefits.

Timon of Athens.   Act I. Sc. 2.

'Tis pity bounty had not eyes behind,
That man might ne'er be wretched for his mind.

Ibid.

For bounty that makes gods, does still mar men.

Act IV.   Sc. 2.

To business that we love we rise betime,
And go to 't with delight.

Antony and Cleopatra.   Act IV. Sc. 4.

For his bounty,
There was no winter in 't; an autumn 't was
That grew the more by reaping.
                                        Act V. Sc. 2.

And the poor beetle that we tread upon,
In corporal sufferance finds a pang as great
As when a giant dies.
                    Measure for Measure.   Act III. Sc. 1.

Where the bee sucks, there suck I;
In a cowslip's bell I lie.
                            Tempest.   Act V. Sc. 1.

Merrily, merrily shall I live now,
Under the blossom that hangs on the bough.
                                        Ibid.

Light boats sail swift, though greater hulks
    draw deep.
                    Troilus and Cressida.   Act II. Sc. 3.

C

Company, villanous company, hath been the
    spoil of me.
                    King Henry IV.   Part I.   Act III. Sc. 3.

Uneasy lies the head that wears a crown.
                        Part II.   Act III. Sc. 1.

A rotten case abides no handling.
                                    Act IV. Sc. 1.

There's a dish of leather coats for you.

Act V. Sc. 3.

It follows then the cat must stay at home.

King Henry V.   Act I. Sc. 2.

The church's prayers made him so prosperous.

King Henry VI.   Part I.   Act I. Sc. 1.

Had not churchmen pray'd
His thread of life had not so soon decay'd.

Ibid.

For friendly counsel cuts off many foes.

King Henry VI.   Part I.   Act III. Sc. 1.

Banish the canker of ambitious thoughts.

King Henry VI.   Part II.   Act I. Sc. 2.

Small curs are not regarded when they grin.

Act III. Sc. 1.

My crown is called content,
A crown it is that seldom kings enjoy.

Part III.   Act. III. Sc. 1.

Deliver all with charity.

King Henry VIII.   Act I. Sc. 2.

Your colt's tooth is not cast yet.

Sc. 3.

'Tis a cruelty
To load a falling man.

Act V. Sc. 3.

Through tatter'd clothes small vices do appear,
Robes and furr'd gowns hide all.
                          King Lear.   Act IV. Sc. 6.

At Christmas I no more desire a rose
Than wish a snow in May's new-fangled mirth.
                  Love's Labour's Lost.   Act I. Sc. 1.

"Past cure is still past care."
                                    Act V. Sc. 2.

Care keeps his watch in every old man's eye,
And where care lodges, sleep will never lie.
                  Romeo and Juliet.   Act II. Sc. 3.

More than prince of cats, I can tell you.
                                          Sc. 4.

'Tis an ill cook that cannot lick his own fingers.
                                    Act IV. Sc. 2.

A countenance more in sorrow than in anger.
                          Hamlet.   Act I. Sc. 2.

A cutpurse of the empire.
                                Act III. Sc. 4.

The cat will mew and dog will have his day.
                                    Act V. Sc. 1.

The crowner hath sat on her, and finds it Christian burial.
                                          Ibid.

A century of prayers.
Cymbeline.   Act IV. Sc. 2.

Good counsellors lack no clients.
Measure for Measure.   Act I. Sc. 2.

Faith, thou hast some crotchets in thy head.
The Merry Wives of Windsor.   Act. II. Sc. 1.

My cake is dough.
Taming of The Shrew.   Act V. Sc. 1.

A harmless necessary cat.
The Merchant of Venice.   Act IV. Sc. 1.

For I am nothing, if not critical.
Othello.   Act II. Sc. 1.

But this denoted a foregone conclusion.
Act III. Sc. 3.

Comparisons are odorous.
Much Ado About Nothing.   Act III. Sc. 5.

Shut up

In measureless content.
Macbeth.   Act II. Sc. 1.

Confusion now hath made his masterpiece.
Act II. Sc. 3.

Two may keep counsel when the third's away.
Titus Andronicus.   Act IV. Sc. 2.

He that will have a cake out of the wheat must
needs tarry the grinding.
Troilus and Cressida.   Act I. Sc. 1.

Ceremony was but devised at first
To set a gloss on faint deeds, hollow welcomes.
Timon of Athens.   Act I. Sc. 2.

This was the most unkindest cut of all.
Julius Cæsar.   Act III. Sc. 2.

Celerity is never more admired
Than by the negligent.
Antony and Cleopatra.   Act III. Sc. 7.

D

It is the disease of not listening, the malady of
  not marking.
King Henry IV.   Part II.   Act I. Sc. 2.

Civil dissension a viperous worm
That gnaws the bowels of the commonwealth.
King Henry VI.   Part I.   Act III. Sc. 1.

Delays have dangerous ends.
Sc. 2.

The gaudy, blabbing and remorseful day
Is crept into the bosom of the sea.
Part II.   Act IV. Sc. 1.

Oh, that deceit should steal such gentle shapes,
And with a virtuous vizard hide foul guile!
King Richard III.   Act II. Sc. 2.

If it were done when 'tis done, then 'twere well
It were done quickly.

Macbeth.   Act I. Sc. 7.

The wealthy curled darlings of our nation.

Othello.   Act I. Sc. 2.

To be once in doubt
Is once to be resolv'd.

Act III. Sc. 3.

A deed without a name.

Act IV. Sc. 1.

It is a good divine that follows his own instructions.

The Merchant of Venice.   Act I. Sc. 2.

There is no darkness but ignorance.

Twelfth Night.   Act IV. Sc. 2.

In the posteriors of this day, which the rude multitude call the afternoon.

Love's Labour's Lost.   Act V. Sc. 1.

The live-long day.

Julius Cæsar.   Act I. Sc. 1.

We burn daylight.

Romeo and Juliet.   Act I. Sc. 4.

These violent delights have violent ends.

Act II. Sc. 6.

Did ever dragon keep so fair a cave?

Act III. Sc. 2.

O, that deceit should dwell
In such a gorgeous palace !

Ibid.

The damned use that word in hell.

Sc. 3.

All difficulties are but easy when they are known.

Measure for Measure. Act IV. Sc. 2.

I must go seek some dew-drops here,
And hang a pearl in every cowslip's ear.

A Midsummer Night's Dream. Act II. Sc. 1.

I must dance barefoot on her wedding day.

Taming of the Shrew. Act II. Sc. 1.

Diseases desperate grown
By desperate appliance are relieved,
Or not at all.

Hamlet. Act IV. Sec. 3.

E

Everything is left at six and seven.
King Richard. Act II. Sc. 2.

Evermore thanks, the exchequer of the poor.
! Sc. 3.

Shall I not take mine ease in mine inn?
King Henry IV. Part I. Act III. Sc. 3.

For now sits Expectation in the air.
King Henry V. Act II. Prologue.

Oft expectation fails and most oft there
Where most it promises.
All's Well That Ends Well. Act II. Sc. 1.

Expectation whirls me round.
Troilus and Cressida. Act III. Sc. 2.

Palsied eld.
Measure for Measure. Act III. Sc. 1.

Will you take eggs for money?
The Winter's Tale. Act I. Sc. 2.

Unless experience be a jewel.
The Merry Wives of Windsor. Act II. Sc. 2.

I have gained my experience.
As You Like It. Act IV. Sc. 1.

The eagle suffers little birds to sing.
Titus Andronicus. Act IV. Sc. 4.

Enough, with over-measure.
>> Coriolanus.   Act III. Sc. 1.

Stabbed with a white wench's black eye.
>> Romeo and Juliet.   Act II. Sc. 4.

The expectancy and rose of the fair state,
The glass of fashion and the mould of form.
>> Hamlet.   Act III. Sc. 1.

I tax not you, you elements, with unkindness.
>> King Lear.   Act III. Sc. 2.

I am dying, Egypt, dying.
>> Antony and Cleopatra.   Act IV. Sc. 15.

Still constant is a wondrous excellence.
>> Sonnet CV.

Now expectation, tickling skittish spirits,
On one and other side.
>> Troilus and Cressida.   Prologue.

F

The ripest fruit first falls.
>> King Richard II.   Act II. Sc. 1.

Violent fires soon burn out themselves.
>> Ibid.

To the latter end of a fray and the beginning of
a feast
Fits a dull fighter and a keen guest.
>> King Henry IV.   Part I.   Act IV. Sc. 2.

Food for powder, food for powder; they 'll fill a
pit as well as better.

Act IV. Sc. 2.

Most forcible Feeble.

Part II.   Act III. Sc. 2.

A little fire is quickly trodden out,
Which, being suffer'd, rivers cannot quench.

King Henry VI.   Part III.   Act IV. Sc. 8.

Sweet flowers are slow and weeds make haste.

King Richard III.   Act II. Sc. 4.

Foundations fly the wretched.

Cymbeline.   Act III. Sc. 6.

Some falls are means the happier to arise.

Cymbeline.   Act IV. Sc. 2.

Hang there like fruit, my soul,
Till the tree die!

Act V. Sc. 5

Fears make devils of cherubins, they never see
truly.

Troilus and Cressida.   Act III. Sc. 2.

Fair is foul, and foul is fair.

Macbeth.   Act I. Sc. 1.

To feed were best at home;
From thence the sauce to meat is ceremony.

Act III. Sc. 4.

Absent thee from felicity awhile.
Hamlet.   Act V. Sc. 2.

Small cheer and great welcome makes a merry feast
The Comedy of Errors.   Act III. Sc. 1.

When fowls have no feathers and fish have no fin.
Ibid.

Friendship 's full of dregs.
Timon of Athens.   Act I. Sc. 2.

Has friendship such a faint and milky heart,
It turns in less than two nights?
Act III. Sc. 1.

He lives in fame that died in virtue's cause.
Titus Andronicus.   Act I. Sc. 1.

At my fingers' ends.
Twelfth Night.   Act I. Sc. 3.

All the learned and authentic fellows.
All's Well That Ends Well.   Act II. Sc. 3.

O, what a goodly outside falsehood hath !
The Merchant of Venice.   Act I. Sc. 3.

G

Some are born great, some achieve greatness and some have greatness thrust upon them.

> Twelfth Night. Act II. Sc. 5.

'Tis not for gravity to play at cherry-pit with Satan.

> Act III. Sc. 4.

Hark, the game is roused!

> Cymbeline. Act III. Sc. 3.

Grace me no grace, and uncle me no uncle.

> Ring Richard II. Act II. Sc. 3.

H

I have sounded the very base-string of humility.

> King Henry IV. Part I. Act II. Sc. 4.

There is a history in all men's lives,
Figuring the nature of the times deceased.

> King Henry IV. Part II. Act III. Sc. 1.

All hell shall stir for this.

> King Henry V. Act V. Sc. 1

But Hercules himself must yield to odds.

> King Henry VI. Part III. Act II. Sc. 1.

True hope is swift and flies with swallows' wings;
Kings it makes gods, and meaner creatures kings.

> King Richard III. Act V. Sc. 2.

To climb steep hills
Requires slow pace at first.

King Henry VIII.   Act I. Sc. 1.

Just as high as my heart.

As You Like It.   Act III. Sc. 2.

His very hair is of the dissembling color.

As You Like It.   Act III. Sc. 4.

But, O, how bitter a thing it is to look into
happiness through another man's eyes !

Act V. Sc. 2.

Rich honesty dwells like a miser,   .   in a poor
house.

Sc. 4.

He is now as valiant as
Hercules that only tells a lie and swears it.

Much Ado About Nothing.   Act IV. Sc. 1.

He that of greatest works is finisher
Oft does them by the weakest minister.

All's Well That Ends Well.   Act II. Sc. 1.

Hanging and wiving goes by destiny.

The Merchant of Venice.   Act II. Sc. 9.

He is well paid that is well satisfied.

Act IV. Sc. 1.

Mine host of the Garter!

Merry Wives of Windsor.   Act I. Sc. 3.

A high hope for a low heaven.
Love's Labour's Lost.   Act **I**. Sc. **1**.

A horse to be ambassador for an ass.
Act III. Sc. 1.

He that is giddy thinks the world turns round.
Taming of the Shrew.   Act V. Sc. 2.

Haste still pays haste, and leisure answers leisure.
Measure for Measure.   Act V. Sc. 1.

Hyperion to a satyr.
Hamlet.   Act I. Sc. 2.

Costly thy habit as thy purse can buy,
But not express'd in fancy, rich, not gaudy.
Sc. 3.

What's Hecuba to him, or he to Hecuba,
That he should weep for her?
Act II. Sc. 2.

To be honest as this world goes, is to be a man
picked out of ten thousand.
Act II. Sc. 2

A hit, a very palpable hit.
Act V. Sc. 2.

Our new heraldry is hands, not hearts.
Othello.   Act III. Sc. 4.

And now let's go hand in hand, not one before
another.
The Comedy of Errors.   Act V. Sc. 1.

He sits 'mongst men like a descended god.
Cymbeline.   Act 1. Sc. 6.

A horse ! a horse ! my kingdom for a horse !
King Richard III.   Act V. Sc. 4.

I

Now would I give a thousand furlongs of sea for
an acre of barren ground.
The Tempest.   Act. I. Sc. 1

I thus neglecting worldly ends, all dedicated
To closeness and the bettering of my mind.
Sc. 2.

I have that within which passeth show;
These but the trappings and the suits of woe.
Hamlet.   Act I. Sc. 2.

I could be bounded in a nutshell, and count myself a king of infinite space, were it not that I
have bad dreams.
Act II. Sc. 2.

"I am Sir Oracle,
And when I ope my lips, let no dog bark!"
The Merchant of Venice. Act I. Sc. 1.

I can easier teach twenty what were good to be done than be one of the twenty to follow mine own teaching.
Sc. 2.

Come, I will fasten on this sleeve of thine;
Thou art an elm . . . I a vine.
The Comedy of Errors. Act II. Sc. 2.

It was Greek to me.
Julius Cæsar. Act I. Sc. 2.

Your If is the only peacemaker;
Much virtue in If.
As You Like It. Act V. Sc. 4.

Beware the Ides of March.
Julius Cæsar. Act III. Sc. 1.

I must hear from thee every day in the hour.
Romeo and Juliet. Act III. Sc. 5.

I am as vigilant as a cat to steal cream.
King Henry IV. Act IV. Sc. 2.

Ignorance is the curse of God.
King Henry VI. Part II. Act IV. Sc. 7.

I have an exposition of sleep come upon me.
Midsummer Night's Dream.   Act IV. Sc. 1.

I'll not budge an inch.
The Taming of the Shrew.   Induction.   Sc. 1.

J

As poor as Job?
The Merry Wives of Windsor.   Act V. Sc. 5.

If he be sick with joy, he'll recover without
physic.
King Henry IV.   Part II.   Act IV. Sc. 5.

Now, by two-headed Janus,
Nature hath framed strange fellows in her time.
The Merchant of Venice.   Act I. Sc. 1.

I am a Jew.   Hath not a Jew eyes?   Hath not
a Jew hands, organs, dimensions, senses, affec-
tions, passions?
Act III. Sc. 1.

I thank thee, Jew, for teaching me that word.
Act IV. Sc. 1.

I am a Jew else, an Ebrew Jew.
King Henry IV.   Part I.   Act II. Sc. 4.

K

What surety of the world, what hope, what stay,
When this was now a king, and now is clay?
King John.   Act V. Sc. 7.

A rascally yea-for-sooth knave.
King Henry IV.   Part II.   Act I. Sc. 2.

Three misbegotten knaves in kendal green.
King Henry IV.   Part I.   Act II. Sc. 4.

The knave is my honest friend, sir, therefore,
I beseech your worship, let him be countenanced.
Part II.   Act V. Sc. 1.

" A crafty knave does need no broker."
King Henry VI.   Part II.   Act I. Sc. 2.

More knave than fool.
King Lear.   Act I. Sc. 4.

Whip me such honest knaves.
Othello.   Act I. Sc. 1.

His kissing is as full of sanctity as the touch
of holy bread.
As You Like It.   Act III. Sc. 4.

A little more than kin and less than kind.
Hamlet.   Act I. Sc. 2.

I must be cruel, only to be kind.
Act III. Sc. 4.

"Now the king drinks to Hamlet."

Act V. Sc. 2.

Yet do I fear thy nature ;
It is too full o' the milk of human kindness.

Macbeth. Act I. Sc. 5.

L

Old father antic the law.

King Henry IV. Part I. Act I. Sc. 2.

More than a little is by much too much.

Act III. Sc. 2.

Lord, Lord, how subject we old men are to this
vice of lying !

Part II. Act III. Sc. 2.

But in these nice sharp quillets of the law,
Good faith, I am no wiser than a daw.

King Henry VI. Part I. Act II. Sc. 4.

Woe to that land that 's govern'd by a child !

King Richard III. Act II. Sc. 3.

A load would sink a navy.

King Henry VIII. Act III. Sc. 2.

A most unspotted lily shall she pass
To the ground, and all the world shall mourn her.

Act V. Sc. 5.

Hark, hark! the lark at heaven's gate sings.
Cymbeline.   Act II. Sc. 2.

The lamb entreats the butcher.
Act III. Sc. 4.

Moderate lamentation is the right of the dead,
extravagant grief the enemy to the living.
All's Well That Ends Well.   Act I. Sc. 1.

No legacy is so rich as honesty.
Act III. Sc. 5.

Still you keep o' the windy side of the law.
Twelfth Night.   Act III. Sc. 4.

As good luck would have it.
The Merry Wives of Windsor.   Act III. Sc. 5.

In law what plea so tainted and corrupt
But, being seasoned with a gracious voice,
Obscures the show of evil?
The Merchant of Venice.   Act III. Sc. 2.

Why, headstrong liberty is lash'd with woe.
The Comedy of Errors.   Act II. Sc. 1.

I have had my labour for my travail.
Troilus and Cressida.   Act I. Sc. 1.

The labour we delight in physics pain.
Macbeth.   Act II. Sc. 3.

M

The memory be green.

Hamlet.   Act I. Sc. 2.

While memory holds a seat
In this distracted globe.

Act I. Sc. 5.

Yea, from the table of my memory
I 'll wipe away all trivial fond records.

Ibid.

Here 's metal more attractive.

Act III. Sc. 2.

To hold, as 'twere, the mirror up to nature.

Ibid.

There 's no art
To find the mind's construction in the face.

Macbeth.   Act I. Sc. 4.

Memory, the warder of the brain.

Sc. 7.

Pour the sweet milk of concord into hell.

Act IV. Sc. 3.

Lay on, Macduff,
And damn'd be him that first cries, " Hold,
enough!"

Macbeth.   Act V. Sc. 8.

Nothing comes amiss, so money comes withal.

The Taming of the Shrew.   Act I. Sc. 2.

'Tis the mind that makes the body rich.

Act IV. Sc. 3.

When maidens sue,
Men give like gods.

Measure for Measure.   Act I. Sc. 4.

The miserable have no other medicine but only hope.

Act III. Sc. 1.

Your marriage comes by destiny.

All's Well That Ends Well.   Act I. Sc. 3.

Now I see
The mystery of your loneliness, and find your salt tears' head.

Ibid.

A young man married is a man that 's marr'd.

Act II. Sc. 3.

You are thought here to be the most senseless and fit man for the constable of the watch.

Much Ado About Nothing.   Act III. Sc. 3.

I have no moral meaning;
I meant, plain holy-thistle.

Sc. 4,

Thou flatter'st misery.

Timon of Athens.   Act IV. Sc. 3.

Willing misery
Outlives incertain pomp.

Ibid.

Put money in thy purse.
Othello.   Act. I. Sc. 3.

A golden mind stoops not to shows of dross.
Merchant of Venice.   Act II. Sc. 7.

And sleep in dull cold marble.
King Henry VIII.   Act III. Sc. 2.

Henceforth my wooing mind shall be express'd
In russet yeas and honest kersey noes.
Love's Labour's Lost.   Act. V. Sc. 2.

Misery acquaints a man with strange bed-fellows.
The Tempest.   Act II. Sc. 2.

Unquiet meals make ill digestions.
The Comedy of Errors.   Act V. Sc. 1

In a minute there are many days.
Romeo and Juliet.   Act III. Sc. 5.

They say if money go before,
All ways do lie open.
Merry Wives of Windsor.   Act II. Sc. 2.

Here's a million of manners.
Two Gentlemen of Verona.   Act II. Sc. 1.

Yea, my memory is tired.
Coriolanus.   Act I. Sc. 9.

N

True nobility is exempt from fear.
King Henry VI.   Part II.   Act IV. Sc. 1.

I am sworn brother   .   .   .
To grim necessity, and he and I
Will keep a league till death.
King Richard II.   Act III. Sc. 1.

They'll not show their teeth in way of smile
Though Nestor swear the jest be laughable.
The Merchant of Venice.   Act I. Sc. 1.

This night methinks is but the daylight sick.
Act V. Sc. I.

Nature teaches beasts to know their friends.
Coriolanus.   Act II. Sc. 1.

The deep of night is crept upon our talk,
And nature must obey necessity.
Julius Cæsar.   Act IV. Sc. 3.

Nothing is
But what is not.
Macbeth.   Act I. Sc. 3.

In them nature's copy 's not eterne.
Act III. Sc. 2.

The night is long that never finds the day.
Act V. Sc. 1.

O

A good mouth-filling oath.
King Henry IV.   Part I.   Act III. Sc. 1.

Order gave each thing view.
King Henry VIII.   Act I. Sc. 1.

I have bought
Golden opinions from all sorts of people.
Macbeth.   Act I. Sc. 2.

Thus ornament is but the guiled shore
To a most dangerous sea.
The Merchant of Venice.   Act III. Sc. 2.

One out of suits with fortune.
As You Like It.   Act I. Sc. 2.

P

And therefore welcome the sour cup of prosperity!
Love's Labour's Lost.   Act 1, Sc. 1.

O me, with what strict patience have I sat,
To see a king transformed to a gnat !
Act IV. Sc. 3.

But most it is presumption in us when
The help of heaven we count the act of men.
All's Well That Ends Well.   Act II. Sc. 1.

From lowest place when virtuous things proceed,
The place is dignified by the doer's deed.

Sc. 3.

Prosperity 's the very bond of love.

The Winter's Tale.   Act IV. Sc. 4.

Much is the force of heaven-bred poesy.

Two Gentlemen of Verona.   Act III. Sc. 2.

How high a pitch his resolution soars !

King Richard II.   Act I. Sc. 1.

Pride must have a fall.

Act V. Sc. 5.

Hide not thy poison with such sugar'd words.

King Henry VI.   Part II.   Act III. Sc. 2.

No man's pie is freed
From his ambitious finger.

King Henry VIII.   Act I. Sc. 1.

He brings his physic
After his patient's death.

Act III. Sc. 2.

Kill thy physician, and the fee bestow
Upon thy foul disease.

King Lear.   Act I. Sc. 1.

Pitchers have ears.

Taming of the Shrew.   Act. IV. Sc. 4.

My purpose is, indeed, a horse of that colour.

Twelfth Night.   Act II. Sc. 3.

The learned pate
Ducks to the golden fool.
                    Timon of Athens.   Act IV. Sc. 3.

At lovers' perjuries,
They say, Jove laughs.
                    Romeo and Juliet.   Act II. Sc. 2.

The flighty purpose never is o'ertook
Unless the deed go with it.
                    Macbeth.   Act IV. Sc. 1.

Throw physic to the dogs; I'll none of it.
                    Act V. Sc. 3.

R

No reckoning made, but, sent to my account
With all my imperfections on my head.
                    Hamlet.   Act I. Sc. 5.

Why, right; you are i' the right.
                    Ibid.

A very riband in the cap of youth.
                    Act IV. Sc. 7.

I am more an antique Roman than a Dane.
                    Act V. Sc. 2.

Romans, countrymen, and lovers! hear me for
my cause, and be silent, that you may hear.
                    Julius Cæsar.   Act III. Sc. 2.

Not that I loved Cæsar less, but that I loved
Rome more.

Ibid.

Friends, Romans, countrymen, lend me your
ears;
I come to bury Cæsar, not to praise him.

Julius Cæsar. Act III. Sc. 2.

This was the noblest Roman of them all.

Act V. Sc. 5.

On the sudden
A Roman thought had struck him.

Antony and Cleopetra. Act I. Sc. 2.

The purest treasure mortal times afford
Is spotless reputation.

King Richard II. Act I. Sc. 1.

In rage deaf as the sea, hasty as fire.

King Richard II. Act I. Sc. 1.

Reputation, reputation, reputation !
O, I have lost my reputation ! I have lost the
immortal part of myself.

Othello. Act II. Sc. 3.

But earthlier happy is the rose distill'd
Than that which withering on the virgin thorn
Grows, lives, and dies in single blessedness.

A Midsummer Night's Dream. Act I. Sc. 1.

To revenge is no valour, but to bear.

Timon of Athens. Act III. Sc. 5.

O, Romeo, Romeo ! wherefore art thou Romeo?
Romeo and Juliet.   Act II. Sc. 2.

The insane root
That takes the reason prisoner.
Macbeth.   Act I. Sc. 3.

S

Bootless speed,
When cowardice pursues and valour flies.
Midsummer Night's Dream.   Act II. Sc. 1.

Out of this silence yet I pick'd a welcome.
Act V. Sc. 1.

Be check'd for silence,
But never tax'd for speech.
All's Well That Ends Well.   Act I. Sc. 1.

Though our silence be drawn from us with cars,
yet peace.
Twelfth Night.   Act II. Sc. 5.

Birm. Things hid and barr'd . . . from com-
mon sense?
King. Ay, that is study's god-like recompense.
Love's Labour's Lost.   Act I. Sc. 1.

Society, saith the text, is the happiness of life.
Act IV. Sc. 2.

I do desire we may be better strangers.
As You Like It.   Act III. Sc. 2.

For sufferance is the badge of all our tribe.
Merchant of Venice. Act I. Sc. 3.

How oft the sight of means to do ill deeds
Make deeds ill done !
King John.   Act IV. Sc. 2.

The setting sun, and music at the close,
As the last taste of sweets, is sweetest last.
King Richard II.   Act II. Sc. 1.

If all the year were playing holidays,
To sport would be tedious as to work.
King Henry IV.   Part I.   Act I. Sc. 2.

Sink or swim.
Sc. 3.

A deal of skimble-skamble stuff.
Act III. Sc. 1.

Two stars keep not their motion in one sphere.
Act V. Sc. 4.

Base is the slave that pays.
King Henry V.   Act II. Sc. 1.

You rub the sore,
When you should bring the plaster.
The Tempest.   Act II. Sc. 1.

Yet, spaniel-like, the more she spurns my love,
The more it grows and fawneth on her still.
The Two Gentlemen of Verona.   Act IV. Sc. 2.

Society is no comfort
To one not sociable.

Cymbeline. Act IV. Sc. 2.

The self-same sun that shines upon his court
Hides not his visage from our cottage.

The Winter's Tale. Act IV. Sc. 4.

I have not kept my square ; but that to come
Shall all be done by the rule.

Antony and Cleopatra. Act II. Sc. 3.

"Where's my serpent of old Nile?"

Antony and Cleopatra. Act I. Sc. 5.

For greatest scandal waits on greatest state.

Lucrece. Line 1006.

Mend your speech a little,
Lest it may mar your fortunes.

King Lear. Act I. Sc. 1.

Then come kiss me, sweet and twenty.

Twelfth Night. Act II. Sc. 3.

I once did hold it, as our statists do,
A baseness to write fair.

Hamlet. Act V. Sc. 2.

Suspicion all our lives shall be stuck full of eyes.

King Henry IV. Part I. Act V. Sc. 2

Suspicion always haunts the guilty mind.

King Henry VI. Part III. Act V. Sc. 6.

T

Truth hath a quiet breast.
King Richard II.   Act I. Sc. 3.

I know a trick worth two of that.
King Henry IV.   Part I.   Act II. Sc. 1.

Mark now, how a plain tale shall put you down.
Sc. 4.

Talkers are no good doers.
King Richard III.   Act I. Sc. 3.

An honest tale speeds best being plainly told.
Act IV. Sc. 4.

Truth loves open dealing.
King Henry VIII.   Act III. Sc. 1.

For aught I see, they are as sick that surfeit
with too much as they that starve with nothing.
The Merchant of Venice.   Act I. Sc. 2.

Truth will come to light; murder can not be hid
long.
Act II. Sc. 2.

The seeming truth which cunning times put on
To entrap the wisest.
The Merchant of Venice.   Act III. Sc. 2.

Hear you this Triton of the minnows?   Mark you
His absolute " shall."
Coriolanus.   Act III. Sc. 1.

Truth 's a dog must to kennel.

King Lear.   Act I. Sc. 4.

For truth is truth

To the end of reckoning.

Measure for Measure.   Act V. Sc. 1.

He draweth out the thread of his verbosity finer than the staple of his argument.

Love's Labour's Lost.   Act V. Sc. 1.

Truth hath better deeds than words to grace it.

The Two Gentlemen of Verona.   Act II. Sc. 2.

If you have tears prepare to shed them now.

Julius Cæsar.   Act III. Sc. 2.

If after every tempest come such calms,
May the winds blow till they have waken'd death!

Othello.   Act II. Sc. 1.

They laugh that win.

Act IV. Sc. 1.

O, teach me how I should forget to think.

Romeo and Juliet.   Act I. Sc. 1.

Wisely and slow; they stumble that run fast.

Act II. Sc. 3.

Thank me no thanking, nor proud me no prouds.

Act III. Sc. 5.

Like one
Who having into truth, by telling of it,
Made such a sinner of his memory,
To credit his own lie.
The Tempest.   Act I. Sc. 2.

And thereby hangs a tale.
As You Like It.   Act II. Sc. 7.

V

The better part of valour is discretion.
King Henry IV.   Part I.   Act V. Sc. 4.

What valour were it, when a cur doth grin,
For one to thrust his hand between his teeth ?
King Henry VI.   Part III.   Act I. Sc. 4.

Her voice was ever soft,
Gentle, and low, an excellent thing in woman.
King Lear.   Act V. Sc. 3.

He's truly valiant that can wisely suffer.
Timon of Athens.   Act III. Sc. 5.

A violet in the youth of primy nature,
Forward, not permanent, sweet, not lasting.
Hamlet.   Act I. Sc. 3.

My ventures are not in one bottom trusted,
Nor to one place.
The Merchant of Venice.   Act I. Sc. 1.

W

The wise deserves a welcome.
Measure for Measure.   Act III. Sc. 1.

What's mine is yours and what is yours is mine.
Act V. Sc. 1.

Blow, blow, thou winter wind,
Thou art not so unkind
As man's ingratitude.
As You Like It.   Act II. Sc. 7.

Answer me in one word.
Act III. Sc. 2.

It is the witness still of excellency
To put a strange face on his own perfection.
Much Ado About Nothing.   Act II. Sc. 3.

Sits the wind in that corner?
Ibid.

This fellow pecks up wit as pigeons pease.
Love's Labour's Lost.   Act V. Sc. 2.

Behold the window of my heart, mine eye.
Ibid.

Wherefore are these things hid?
Twelfth Night.   Act I. Sc. 3.

O thou invisible spirit of wine, if thou hast no name to be known by, let us call thee devil!

Othello. Act III. Sc. 3.

Every puny whipster.

Act V. Sc. 2.

Wishers were ever fools.

Antony and Cleopatra. Act IV. Sc. 13.

One that loves a cup of hot wine with not a drop of allaying Tiber in 't.

Coriolanus. Act II. Sc. 1.

Come not within the measure of my wrath.

The Two Gentlemen of Verona. Act V. Sc. 4.

Full oft we see
Cold wisdom waiting on superfluous folly.

All's Well That Ends Well. Act I. Sc. 1.

Wealth is burden of my wooing dance.

Taming of the Shrew. Act I. Sc. 2.

Well, if my wind were but long enough to say my prayers, I would repent.

The Merry Wives of Windsor. Act IV. Sc. 5.

The smallest worm will turn being trodden on.

King Henry VI. Part III. Act II. Sc. 2.

Ill blows the wind that profits nobody.

Sc. 5.

Welcome ever smiles,
And farewell goes out sighing.

Troilus and Cressida.   Act III. Sc. 3.

A word and a blow.

Romeo and Juliet.   Act III. Sc. 1.

'Tis lack of kindly warmth they are not kind.

Timon of Athens.   Act II. Sc. 2.

" We have seen better days."

Act IV. Sc. 2.

APPENDIX

Our revels now are ended. These our actors,
As I foretold you, were all spirits, and
Are melted into air, into thin air:
And, like the baseless fabric of this vision,
The cloud-capped towers, the gorgeous palaces,
The solemn temples, the great globe itself,
Yea, all which it inherit, shall dissolve,
And, like this insubstantial pageant faded,
Leave not a rack behind. We are such stuff
As dreams are made on; and our little life
Is rounded with a sleep.
The Tempest.   Act IV. Sc. 1.

She is mine own,
And I as rich in having such a jewel
As twenty seas, if all their sand were pearl,
The water nectar, and the rocks pure gold.
The Two Gentlemen of Verona.   Act II. Sc. 4.

He makes sweet music with th' enamell'd stones,
Giving a gentle kiss to every sedge
He overtaketh in his pilgrimage.
Sc. 7.

Thyself and thy belongings
Are not thine own so proper as to waste
Thyself upon thy virtues, they on thee.
Heaven doth with us, as we with torches do,
Not light them for themselves; for if our virtues
Did not go forth of us, 'twere all alike
As if we had them not. Spirits are not finely
  touch'd
But to fine issues, nor Nature never lends
The smallest scruple of her excellence
But, like a thrifty goddess, she determines
Herself the glory of a creditor.

Measure for Measure. Act I. Sc. 1.

No ceremony that to great ones 'longs
Not the king's crown, nor the deputed sword,
The marshal's truncheon, nor the judge's robe,
Become them with one-half so good a grace
As mercy does.

Act II. Sc. 2.

Why, all the souls that were were forfeit once;
And He that might the vantage best have took
Found out the remedy. How would you be,
If He, which is the top of judgment, should
But judge you as you are?

Ibid.

But man, proud man,
Drest in a little brief authority,
Most ignorant of what he's most assured,

His glassy essence, like an angry ape,
Plays such fantastic tricks before high heaven
As make the angels weep.

Ibid.

The rude sea grew civil at her song.
And certain stars shot madly from their spheres
To hear the sea-maid's music.

A Midsummer Night's Dream.   Act II. Sc. 1.

And the imperial votaress passed on,
In maiden meditation, fancy-free.
Yet mark'd I where the bolt of Cupid fell;
It fell upon a little western flower,
Before milk-white, now purple with love's wound,
And maidens call it love-in-idleness.

Ibid.

I know a bank where the wild thyme blows,
Where oxlips and the nodding violet grows,
Quite over-canopied with luscious woodbine,
With sweet musk-roses and with eglantine.

Ibid.

The lover, all as frantic,
Sees Helen's beauty in a brow of Egypt:
The poet's eye in a fine frenzy rolling,
Doth glance from heaven to earth, from earth to
    heaven;
And as imagination bodies forth
The forms of things unknown, the poet's pen

Turns them to shapes, and gives to airy nothing
A local habitation and a name.
Such tricks hath strong imagination,
That if it would but apprehend some joy,
It comprehends some bringer of that joy;
Or in the night, imagining some fear,
How easy is a bush supposed a bear!

Act V. Sc. 1.

All things that are
Are with more spirit chased than enjoy'd.
How like a younker or a prodigal
The scarfed bark puts from her native bay,
Hugg'd and embraced by the strumpet wind!
How like the prodigal doth she return,
With over-weather'd ribs and ragged sails,
Lean, rent, and beggar'd by the strumpet wind!

The Merchant of Venice.   Act II. Sc. 6.

I am a Jew.   Hath not a Jew eyes? Hath not
a Jew hands, organs, dimensions, senses, affec-
tions, passions?

Act III. Sc. 1.

The villainy you teach me I will execute, and it
shall go hard, but I will better the instruction.

Ibid.

In law, what plea so tainted and corrupt
But being season'd with a gracious voice
Obscures the show of evil?

Sc. 2.

You call me misbeliever, cutthroat, dog,
And spit upon my Jewish gaberdine.

The Merchant of Venice.   Act I. Sc. 3.

O father Abram! What these Christians are,
Whose own hard dealings teaches them suspect
The thoughts of others!

Act I. Sc. 3.

The quality of mercy is not strain'd,
It droppeth as the gentle rain from heaven
Upon the place beneath.   It is twice blest:
It blesseth him that gives and him that takes.
'T is mightiest in the mightiest: it becomes
The throned monarch better than his crown;
His sceptre shows the force of temporal power,
The attribute to awe and majesty,
Wherein doth sit the dread and fear of kings;
But mercy is above this sceptred sway,
It is enthroned in the hearts of kings,
It is an attribute to God himself;
And earthly power doth then show likest God's
When mercy seasons justice.   Therefore, Jew,
Though justice be thy plea, consider this,
That in the course of justice none of us
Should see salvation; we do pray for mercy;
And that same prayer doth teach us all to render
The deeds of mercy.

Act IV. Sc. 1.

How sweet the moonlight sleeps upon this bank!
Here we will sit and let the sounds of music
Creep in our ears; soft stilness and the night
Become the touches of sweet harmony.
Sit . . . Look how the floor of heaven
Is thick inlaid with patines of bright gold;
There's not the smallest orb which thou behold'st
But in his motion like an angel sings,
Still quiring to the young-eyed cherubins.
Such harmony is in immortal souls;
But whilst this muddy vesture of decay
Doth grossly close it in, we can not hear it.
                                        Act V. Sc. 1.

Sweet are the uses of adversity,
Which like the toad, ugly and venomous,
Wears yet a precious jewel in his head;
And this our life, exempt from public haunt,
Finds tongues in trees, books in running brooks,
Sermons in stones, and good in everything.
                        As You Like It.   Act II. Sc. 1.

          All the world's a stage,
And all the men and women merely players;
They have their exits and their entrances;
And one man in his time plays many parts,
His acts being seven ages.   At first the infant,
Mewling and puking in the nurse's arms.
And then the whining school-boy, with his
    satchel

And shining morning face, creeping like snail
Unwillingly to school. And then the lover,
Sighing like furnace, with a woeful ballad
Made to his mistress' eyebrow. Then a soldier,
Full of strange oaths and bearded like the pard;
Jealous in honour, sudden and quick in quarrel,
Seeking the bubble reputation
Even in the cannon's mouth. And then the
  justice,
In fair round belly, with good capon lined,
With eyes severe and beard of formal cut,
Full of wise saws and modern instances;
And so he plays his part. The sixth age shifts
Into the lean and slipper'd pantaloon,
With spectacles on nose and pouch on side;
His youthful hose, well saved, a world too wide
For his shrunk shank; and his big manly voice,
Turning again toward childish treble, pipes
And whistles in his sound. Last scene of all,
That ends this strange eventful history,
Is second childishness and mere oblivion
Sans teeth, sans eyes, sans taste, sans everything.

As You Like It. Act II. Sc. 7.

The Retort Courteous; . . . the Quip Modest; . . .
  the Reply Churlish; . . . the Reproof Valient;
  . . . the Counter check Quarrelsome; . . .
  the Lie with Circumstance; . . . the Lie Direct.

Act V. Sc. 4.

Look in the chronicles; we came in with Richard
  Conqueror.

> The Taming of the Shrew. Induction. Sc. 1.

If music be the food of love, play on;
Give me excess of it, that, surfeiting,
The appetite may sicken, and so die.
That strain again! it had a dying fall:
Oh, it came o'er my ear like the sweet sound
That breathes upon a bank of violets,
Stealing and giving odour.

> Twelfth Night. Act I. Sc. 1.

Duke.   And what 's her history?
Vio. A blank, my lord. She never told her love,
But let concealment, like a worm i' the bud,
Feed on her damask cheek; she pined in thought,
And with a green and yellow melancholy
She sat like patience on a monument,
Smiling at grief.

> Act II. Sc. 4.

                              What you do
Still betters what is done. When you speak
  sweet,
I 'd have you do it ever; when you sing,
I 'd have you buy and sell so, so give alms,
Pray so; and for the ordering your affairs,
To sing them, too; when you do dance, I wish
  you

A wave o' the sea, that you might ever do
Nothing but that, move still, still so,
And own no other function; each your doing,
So singular in each particular,
Crowns what you are doing in the present deed,
That all your acts are queens.

The Winter's Tale.   Act IV. Sc. 4.

To gild refined gold, to paint the lily,
To throw a perfume on the violet,
To smooth the ice, or add another hue
Unto the rainbow, or with taper light
To seek the beauteous eye of heaven to garnish,
Is wasteful and ridiculous excess.

King John.   Act IV. Sc. 2.

Oh, who can hold a fire in his hand
By thinking on the frosty Caucasus?
Or cloy the hungry edge of appetite
By bare imagination of a feast?
Or wallow naked in December snow
By thinking on fantastic summer's heat?
Oh, no! the apprehension of the good
Gives but the greater feeling to the worse.

King Richard II.   Act I. Sc. 3.

By heaven, methinks it were an easy leap
To pluck bright honour from the pale-faced
moon,
Or dive into the bottom of the deep,

Where fathom-line could never touch the ground,
And pluck up drowned honour by the locks.
King Henry IV.   Part I.   Act I. Sc. 3.

I have peppered two of them, two I am sure I have
paid, two rogues in buckram suits. I tell thee
what, Hal, if I tell thee a lie, spit in my face;
call me horse. Thou knowest my old word:
here I lay, and thus I bore my point. Four
rogues in buckram let drive at me.
Act II. Sc. 4.

Three misbegotten knaves in Kendal green.
Ibid.

Give you a reason on compulsion! if reasons
were as plentiful as blackberries, I would give
no man a reason upon compulsion, I.
King Henry IV.   Part I.   Act II. Sc. 4.

A plague of sighing and grief ! It blows a man
up like a bladder.
Ibid.

Farewell! a long farewell, to all my greatness!
This is the state of man: to-day he puts forth
The tender leaves of hope; to-morrow blossoms,
And bears his blushing honours thick upon him;
The third day comes a frost, a killing frost,
And when he thinks, good easy man, full surely
His greatness is a-ripening, nips his root,
And then he falls, as I do.   I have ventured,

Like little wanton boys that swim on bladders,
This many summers in a sea of glory,
But far beyond my depth: my high-blown pride
At length broke under me and now has left me,
Weary and old with service, to the mercy
Of a rude stream, that must forever hide me.
Vain pomp and glory of this world, I hate ye:
I feel my heart new opened. Oh how wretched
Is that poor man that hangs on princes' favours!
There is betwixt that smile we would aspire to
That sweet aspect of princes, and their ruin,
More pangs and fears than wars or women have:
And when he falls, he falls like Lucifer,
Never to hope again.
> King Henry VIII.   Act III. Sc. 2.

Love thyself last: cherish those hearts that hate
    thee;
Corruption wins not more than honesty,
Still in thy right hand carry gentle peace,
To silence envious tongues.   Be just, and fear
    not:
Let all the ends thou aims't at be thy country's,
Thy God's, and truth's; then if thou fall'st . . .
Thou fall'st a blessed martyr!
> King Henry VIII.   Act III. Sc. 3.

Immortal gods I crave no pelf;
I pray for no man but myself;
Grant I may never prove so fond,
To trust man on his oath or bond.
> Timon of Athens.   Act I. Sc. 2.

Ye gods, it doth amaze me
A man of such a feeble temper should
So get the start of the majestic world
And bear the palm alone.
                    Julius Cæsar.   Act I. Sc. 2.

Why, man, he doth bestride the narrow world
Like a Colossus, and we petty men
Walk under his huge legs and peep about
To find ourselves dishonourable graves.
Men at some time are masters of their fates;
The fault, dear Brutus, is not in our stars,
But in ourselves, that we are underlings.
                                        Ibid.

Romans, countrymen, and lovers! hear me for
my cause, and be silent, that you may hear:
believe me for mine honour, and have respect
to mine honour, that you may believe; censure
me in your wisdom, and awake your senses,
that you may the better judge.

.   .   .   .

Not that I loved Cæsar less, but that I loved
Rome more.
                            Act III. Sc. 2.

Friends, Romans, countrymen, lend me your ears;
I come to bury Cæsar, not to praise him.
The evil that men do lives after them;
The good is oft interred with their bones;

So let it be with Cæsar.   The noble Brutus
Hath told you Cæsar was ambitious:
If it were so, it was a grievous fault,
And grievously hath Cæsar answer'd it.
Here, under leave of Brutus and the rest—
For Brutus is an honourable man;
So are they all, all honourable men—
Come I to speak in Cæsar's funeral.
He was my friend, faithful and just to me;
But Brutus says he was ambitious;
And Brutus is an honourable man.
He hath brought many captives home to Rome,
Whose ransoms did the general coffers fill:
Did this in Cæsar seem ambitious?
When that the poor have cried, Cæsar hath wept:
Ambition should be made of sterner stuff:
Yet Brutus says he was ambitious;
And Brutus is an honourable man.
You all did see that on the Lupercal
I thrice presented him a kingly crown
Which he did thrice refuse: was this ambition?
Yet Brutus says he was ambitious;
And, sure, he is an honourable man.
I speak not to disprove what Brutus spoke,
But here I am to speak what I do know.
You all did love him once, not without cause:
What cause withholds you then, to mourn for him?
O judgment! thou art fled to brutish beasts,
And men have lost their reason.

Ibid.

Methought I heard a voice cry, "Sleep no more!
Macbeth doth murder sleep!" the innocent sleep,
Sleep that knits up the ravell'd sleave of care,
The death of each day's life, sore labour's bath,
Balm of hurt minds, great nature's second course,
Chief nourisher in life's feast.

Macbeth.   Act II. Sc. 2.

Thou canst not say I did it; never shake
Thy gory locks at me.

Macbeth.   Act III. Sc. 4.

The time has been,
That when the brains were out the man would
 die,
And there an end; but now they rise again,
With twenty mortal murders on their crowns,
And push us from our stools.

Ibid.

My way of life
Is fall'n into the sere, the yellow leaf;
And that which should accompany old age,
As honour, love, obedience, troops of friends,
I must not look to have; but in their stead
Curses, not loud but deep, mouth-honour, breath,
Which the poor heart would fain deny, and dare
 not.

Macbeth.   Act V. Sc. 3.

Cure her of that.
Canst thou not minister to a mind diseas'd,
Pluck from the memory a rooted sorrow,
Raze out the written troubles of the brain,
And with some sweet oblivious antidote
Cleanse the stuff'd bosom of that perilous stuff
Which weighs upon the heart?

Ibid.

To-morrow, and to-morrow, and to-morrow,
Creeps in this petty pace from day to day
To the last syllable of recorded time,
And all our yesterdays have lighted fools
The way to dusty death.   Out, out, brief candle!
Life's but a walking shadow, a poor player
That struts and frets his hour upon the stage
And then is heard no more: it is a tale
Told by an idiot, full of sound and fury,
Signifying nothing.

Macbeth.   Act V. Sc. 5.

In the most high and palmy state of Rome,
A little ere the mightiest Julius fell,
The graves stood tenantless, and the sheeted dead
Did squeak and gibber in the Roman streets.

Hamlet.   Act I. Sc. I.

Seems, Madam! nay, it is; I know not " seems."
'Tis not alone my inky cloak, good mother,
Nor customary suits of solemn black.

Sc. 2.

But I have that within which passeth show;
These but the trappings and the suits of woe.

Ibid.

Hyperion to a satyr; so loving to my mother,
That he might not beteem the winds of heaven
Visit her face too roughly.

Ibid.

Do not, as some ungracious pastors do,
Show me the steep and thorny way to heaven;
Whiles, like a puff'd and reckless libertine,
Himself the primrose path of dalliance treads,
And recks not his own rede.

Hamlet.   Act I. Sc. 3.

Be thou familiar, but by no means vulgar.
Those friends thou hast, and their adoption tried,
Grapple them to thy soul with hoops of steel.

Ibid.

Beware

Of entrance to a quarrel; but being in,
Bear 't that the opposed may beware of thee.
Give every man thy ear, but few thy voice;
Take each man's censure, but reserve thy judg-
      ment.
Costly thy habit as thy purse can buy,
But not express'd in fancy, rich, not gaudy.
For the apparal oft proclaims the man.

Ibid.

Neither a borrower nor a lender be;
For loan oft loses both itself and friend,
And borrowing dulls the edge of husbandry.
This above all: to thine own self be true,
And it must follow, as the night the day,
Thou canst not then be false to any man.

Ibid.

This goodly frame, the earth, seems to me a
sterile promontory; this most excellent canopy,
the air, look you, this brave o'erhanging firma-
ment, this majestical roof fretted with golden
fire, why, it appears no other thing to me than
a foul and pestilent congregation of vapours.
What a piece of work is a man! how noble in
reason! how infinite in faculty! in form and
moving how express and admirable! in action
how like an angel! in apprehension how like a
god!

Act II. Sc. 2.

To be, or not to be; that is the question:
Whether 'tis nobler in the mind to suffer
The slings and arrows of outrageous fortune,
Or to take arms against a sea of troubles,
And by opposing end them? To die: to sleep:
No more; and by a sleep to say we end
The heartache and the thousand natural shocks

That flesh is heir to—'tis a consummation
Devoutly to be wish'd.   To die, to sleep;
To sleep; perchance to dream: ay, there's the
      rub:
For in that sleep of death what dreams may come,
When we have shuffled off this mortal coil,
Must give us pause: there's the respect
That makes calamity of so long life;
For who would bear the whips and scorns of time,
The oppressor's wrong, the proud man's con-
      tumely,
The pangs of dispised love, the law's delay,
The insolence of office and the spurns
That patient merit of the unworthy takes,
When he himself might his quietus make
With a bare bodkin? Who would fardels bear,
To grunt and sweat under a weary life,
But that the dread of something after death,
The undiscover'd country from whose bourn
No traveller returns, puzzles the will
And makes us rather bear those ills we have
Than fly to others that we know not of?
Thus conscience does make cowards of us all;
And thus the native hue of resolution
Is sicklied o'er with the pale cast of thought,
And enterprises of great pith and moment
With this regard their currents turn awry,
And lose the name of action.

                          Act III. Sc. 1.

There is a special providence in the fall of a
sparrow. If it be now, 't is not to come ; if it
be not to come, it will be now ; if it be not
now, yet it will come : the readiness is all.
Since no man has aught of what he leaves,
what is 't to leave betimes?

Act V. Sc. 2.

This is the excellent foppery of the world that,
when we are sick in fortune,—often the surfeit
of our own behaviour,—we make guilty of our
disasters the sun, the moon, and the stars; as
if we were villains by necessity; fools by
heavenly compulsion; knaves, thieves, and
treachers by spherical predominance; drunk-
ards, liars, and adulterers, by an enforced obedience of planetary influence; and all that we are
evil in, by a divine thrusting on: . . . to lay
his goatish disposition to the charge of a star!

King Lear.   Act I. Sc. 2.

Poor naked wretches, wheresoe'er you are,
That bide the pelting of this pitiless storm,
How shall your houseless heads and unfed sides,
Your looped and windowed raggedness, defend
you
From seasons such as these?

Act III. Sc. 4.

A man may see how this world goes with no eyes.
Look with thine ears; see how yond justice rails

upon yond simple thief. Hark, in thine ear: change places; and, handy-dandy, which is the justice, which is the thief?

Act IV. Sc. 6.

Most potent, grave, and reverend signiors,
My very noble and approv'd good masters,
That I have ta'en away this old man's daughter,
It is most true: 1 have married her:
The very head and front of my offending
Hath this extent, no more. Rude am I in my speech,
And little bless'd with the soft phrase of peace:
For since these arms of mine had seven years' pith,
Till now some nine moons wasted, they have used
Their dearest action in the tented field,
And little of this great world can I speak
More than pertains to feats of broil and battle,
And therefore little shall I grace my cause
In speaking for myself. Yet, by your gracious patience,
I will a round unvarnished tale deliver
Of my whole course of love.

Othello. Act I. Sc. 3.

Her father loved me; oft invited me;
Still question'd me the story of my life
From year to year, the battles, sieges, fortunes,
That I have passed.

Ibid.

WS - #0213 - 110423 - C0 - 229/152/10 - PB - 9781331759911 - Gloss Lamination